MUSIC AT THE HEART OF THINKING

ALSO BY FRED WAH

and published by Talonbooks

beholden: a poem as long as the river with Rita Wong

is a door

Scree: The Collected Earlier Poems, 1962–1991

Selected Poems: Loki Is Buried at Smoky Creek

Sentenced to Light

MUSIC AT THE HEART OF THINKING

IMPROVISATIONS 1–170

FRED WAH

TALONBOOKS

Talonbooks
9259 Shaughnessy Street, Vancouver, British Columbia, Canada V6P 6R4
talonbooks.com

Talonbooks is located on xʷməθkʷəy̓əm, Sḵwx̱wú7mesh, and səlilwətaʔɬ Lands.

First printing: 2020

Typeset in Futura
Printed and bound in Canada on 100% post-consumer recycled paper

Interior and cover design by Typesmith

Talonbooks acknowledges the financial support of the Canada Council for the Arts, the
Government of Canada through the Canada Book Fund, and the Province of British
Columbia through the British Columbia Arts Council and the Book Publishing Tax Credit.

Library and Archives Canada Cataloguing in Publication

Title: Music at the heart of thinking. Improvisations 1–170 / Fred Wah.
Names: Wah, Fred, 1939– author.
Description: Improvisations 1–69 previously published under title: Music at the heart of
thinking. Red Deer, Alberta: Red Deer College Press, 1987. | Improvisations 70–105
previously published under title: Alley alley home free. Red Deer, Alberta: Red Deer
College Press, 1992. | Poems. |
   Includes index.
Identifiers: Canadiana 20200225146 | ISBN 9781772012620 (softcover)
Classification: LCC PS8545.A28 M87 2020 | DDC C811/.54—dc23

So long as the sky is recognized as an association

is recognized in its function of accessory to vague words
    whose meaning it is impossible to rediscover
its value can be nothing but mathematical certain limits of
    gravity and density of air

—**William Carlos Williams**
    Spring and All (1923)

One makes (the) difference

To say: "I don't understand what this means," is, at least, to recognize that "this" means. The problem is that meaning is not a totality of sameness and predictability. Within each word, each sentence, meaning has slipped a little out of sight and all we have are traces, shadows, still warm ashes. The meaning available from language goes beyond the actual instance of this word, that word. A text is a place where a labyrinth of continually revealing meanings are available, a place that offers more possibility than we can be sure we know, sometimes more than we want to know. It isn't a container, static and apparent. Rather, it is noisy, frequently illegible. Reading into meaning starts with a questioning glance, a seemingly obvious doubloon on a mast. The multiplicity can be read, should be read, even performed. But then again, perhaps meaning is intransitive and unreadable, only meant to be made. No sooner do we name meaning than it dissipates. As a sure thing, it eludes us. It arouses us to attempt an understanding, to interpret. But this is usually unsatisfying since whatever direction we approach from only leads us to suspect there is no one direction. No single meaning is the right one because no "right ones" stand still long enough to get caught. But because we do not know does not mean we are lost. Something that's strangely familiar, not quite what we expect, but familiar, is present. That quick little gasp in the daydream, a sudden sigh of recognition, a little sock of baby breath. Writing into meaning starts at the white page, nothing but intention. This initial blinding clarity needs to be disrupted before we're tricked into settling for a staged and diluted paradigm of the "real," the good old familiar, inherited, understandable, unmistakable lucidity of phrase that feels safe and sure, a simple sentence, just-like-the-last-time sentence. One makes (the) difference. Meaning generates and amplifies itself, beyond itself, but never forgets; fragments of its memory and its potency exceed itself with meaning full of desire and can only be found hiding between the words and lines and in a margin large enough for further thought, music at the heart of thinking, go ahead

1

Don't think thinking without heart no such separation
within the acting body takes a step without all of it the self
propelled into doing the thing (for example, the horse) and
on the earth as well picking up the whole circuit feet first feel
the waves tidal and even outside to moon and sun it's OK
to notate only one of those things without knowing fixed
anyway some heart sits in the arms of

Preact the mind ahead of the writing but stop to think
notation of the mind ahead pre-tell the "hunt" message
doesn't run like the wind like makes it believe wild
imagination or trees or animals too to preface the head
ahead but notice the body as a drummer pre-acts the hands
to do to do insistent so it can come out tah dah at every
point simply the mind at work won't do or the body minding
itself thinking (which is why the drum's made from cedar) get
it right or get it wrong like strike from the body falling back
thoughts fall behind to the notes sometimes gives it shape as
body hits my drum tah dum

3

Wait for the mind to stop for the writing to go ahead into
the rush for the hand to hold the head's waiting (or keep the
motor running) in place of caught movement of world art
at a standstill picture I thought to write to move could be a
movement of the movement Fenollosa naturally more music
in the body heaves the mind to work inside the body syntax
synapse to jump the spot or specific junction shipped into
the text with the mind caught thinking earth earthing world
world music a sign aptic rhythm of body convulsion call it
proprioception or call it desire but only override the "eme"
with something there something factual the "ing" always
inging for instance like S said of the grapheme saying it into
the page living and longing keeps (the baseball in there
somewhere) invisible visible

3.1

The happy lady and the bird 1949 or maybe some boomerang of a dark blue moon's always been life with chalk Joan's muttered words on the sidewalk scotched plan fresh game ahead hop slope and tree the flyball inside old catalogue mitt such sign as stone thrown to box fetter counting with wishes on sky dome

4

To take apart the tree bark by bark and burn it up top to
keep the skin spread open to the air that moves through
the world-tree message seems unnoticeable capable to the
area over which limbs cover all those upright configurations
for the connection between branches and roots likewise any
surface to depth genetics provides unmentionable because
invisible soundings taken quickly re the mouthings of the
trembling body another language like French might place
elsewhere simple as tongue there is after all reaching for the
water, reaching for the sun

4.1

Yet another picture of tree I think opened up forests of
thought or trees maybe by washed out glaze simply making
outline eyes half closed remembering some truth tree made
up of many nor not sure colour could do it water underneath
all surfaces enlarged touched hut of my mind literal no-name
watercolour simple yet suggested and entered old fallen
tamarack Helen limb peeling itself back into same earth

4.2

from the ceiling
full of "heart." Nana

why not
sneeze again Duchamp

in 1954 my father's car
coming and going

I remember phanopoeia's casting
getting into Jon Whyte's Banff

when you are 24 your
"Trees" are everything

5

Put there to indicate nothing necessarily but its own possible
dimensions from everywhere else that it simply participate in
the flow fish as vector some Platonic creek homing in on the
spawn of itself or probably "emeness" of the world to hold
all writing actually in motion witnessable to both river and
salmon one can't know the individual ocean's accumulation
to ward off the trace or the containing container of the
"universe" could change at a touch the guideline-point or
hologrammar effect what'd he say not just dual but "four
steps: negative/positive (forward) & negative/positive
(backward), or no-yes/no-yes" not as a grid not as a plan
but at every single point a part of the whole picture down to
the very piece of gravel we believe in the water, the egg

6

Sentence the true morphology or shape of the mind
including a complete thought forever little ridges little
rhythms scoping out the total picture as a kind of automatic
designing device or checklist anyone I've found in true
thought goes for all solution to the end concatenates every
component within the lines within the picture as a cry to
represent going to it with the definite fascination of a game
where the number of possibilities increases progressively
with each additional bump Plato thought

7

Repetition by nature desire and need becomes a relief or by jargon animals again and again feeding themselves in the substrate forest naturally unaccented up beat figure it out stone outlives the message preserve and disseminate the single solely by the light and shade hemisphere disappearance of the material self simply in order to understand or learn since the "sieve" or "colander" is only rational some Chinese invention in syncopation usually a beam technique foraging with the mule in the sunlight now more than ever you need a copying device undreamed-of switching hungry for the next beat

8

Prevention of the feeling out by previous sets "I" gets
enclosed again except by stealth to find the point where
Harrison says *dromenon* pre-tells story being dangerously
easy to repeat (all the time) but "L" or "P" or like Nicole
in her book or even the bible are new once just about
accidental why stumbling is not taught in the court everyone
else believes in animals too to fake writing just like Shao
Lin under the moon the drunk dance *ostranenie* via K., K.,
and Shklovsky making strange eyes half-closed negative
capability defamiliar estranged and abstract cover trade
nothing for another otherwise imposed logic but watch it
if you think there is an edge then swim or climb maybe the
drunkenness of a foreign dance or sentence saying this

8.1

Take anything Max Ernst you fish as much as the birds eyes
horses so the eyes are the same the eyes are not always the
same look right into the wood like heart right? say through
plaster-cast dactyllic to feel in a knot eyes and in the wood
eyes out of the wood or a figure cut from *Un Chinois égaré*
A Lost (Bewildered) Chinaman he called it natural history
you can imagine the silk print since youth stare at things
at any things

9

Memory behind the fingers too remember the stove's hot thus
numbers right the surplus substance coded as braille at the
tips still a stage further than the mind the dot there but taken
in the rush forward to the surface as revibration orthography
sticks in our craw alphabet is all an act but not the one
behind memory or numerical value if you've never ridden a
horse grammar is there for that if you forget hold on

10

Now I get to hear the language rather than only see it in
French over my head fingers want to touch the sight of the
letter oral tactile fragment hunger in another language
the wolf's ear to make it up before it happens to hear
it somewhere inside my body before the lips touch the
mouthpiece or fingertip valves as soft as silk intelligence like
that gets carried in the language by itself the cow simply
eats the whole field I have to practice to get it right

11

Ongoing dialogue in between surfaces and fields middle-voice dipolar action done for the one self speaking within or to the skin via rhythm image to know sheet music as in Japanese counted morphologically like an idea and then used Marx (Mars) for currency movement to the instrument or bicameral tumblers sparked shock wave blip simple breathing of the magnetic dip

ANOTHER MHT

Once thinking as feeling thought
then becomes simple and above
crows fly in no pattern
wounding the fibres through fir and spruce, already
system takes over voice
today was beautiful, clear, crisp, the trees
expect nothing if not imprint or pre-print of
time so surrounds all the birds' caw's last name
swoops through the air with feather,
snow to not know "the silent life"
soft earth, guttural
what I mean is the quick body
as it comes to the throat like that

12

Don't really write just work with it after it arrives Joanne
Gerber says total she and my bodies in candida alert across
the prairies with practice hit my world and stomach look for
the speaking language speaking another language as in
the music driven body horn hopes to push minding my own
what I need is a piece of wire or a Japanese word to make
yummy thinking keep up with the electricity but voice of
voices American watches out for such a line Site "C" maybe
Caroline will string it in "Keeping the Peace" or what if it was
French as in Qu'Appelle

13

I wish for the osprey nest getting this just like a letter to
Gerry I could have it habited on this hilltop wheat field
plateau me like a boat going off in three directions with
the wind minding the bike both with and against it and the
swirling summer dust and chaff devils in Swift Current bring
water to a gopher hole lacrosse is like that as a kind of
medicine I mean game just sleeplessness laying low in the
heartland very few numbers to work with here yet I like the
diving craze Sally got by asking a question writ silence back
into the flat whoosh and rumble I can't sleep under coming
at me over the whole northern stretch to the ice cap when I
did tai chi this morning a squirrel fell asleep watching me in
the pine limb above my head take that and push it into the
buttock and shoulder there is no elegy here things'll have
to be different if the bird and kinetic glacier know anything
'bout what they're up to I hope

13.1

Schumann resonance frequencies the earth
our hearts harmonize seven
point eight per second
the neuron horizon

circles the lake-nests
osprey gone, the burning season
hub of pilings, hub of water
the day hue fades, buzzes

to stop fish this port closed
still shudder but lap lap bough hanged
summer
bark

14

Try all the objects/people except speed the/my mind or
morning which will merely lock into the heart for editing train
after train so I don't think knowing will tell you rock along
the beach meaning tries to be everything just like eccles
cakes are sweet especially with butter but then sighing does
just what you want/need how to sharpen those Chinese
exercises or match the pebble eating its world even the
river gets into the lake as thought skipped over the surface
counting and then sinks but there's the arm sinking too simply
from habit that's perfect clarity things around us plus persons
and places Vancouver maybe a little Italian lunacy shades of
Prague watch Rodefer carefully essaying how symbol clouds
the sky yet signs the size of sandwiches or granodiorite
rocks we dive from pool into those same canyons migration
of the soul i.e. ocean and maps of trailing training currents
currants

15

O no! Sunlight suddenly on the patio steps and I'm in a
Kyoto temple persistence of the spirit sometimes turns
root words without mathematics and without visible profile
the true face of a two-faced man *le vrai visage* etcetera I
catch myself in place and the moment shines maybe a little
like "scrub lake" queued for the printout along the shore
everyone is busy in their summer palaces it's hot and dry in
the hills I write this to you in the Shanghai dialect Mori-san
your eyes answer me with the word for sunlight please

16

otherwise;
right now it's confusing.

small words
small months
announcements, abandonments
and tribulations; tell me.

raptures now risks, secret
parts —
nervous falcons.

shy shit;
materials, circumstances,
that's for sure.

that's what we'll miss.

an abolition of another longing.

17

sea liquid is endomorphic red
ochre imprint for that self
it intervenes as a shadow on this planet
the skin and the wall, all these reappearances
all these others, and then birth with a life
like one of your long novels
jellyfish evaporated, fell back
the urgent life was full of opacity
my old felt hat got wet and muggy
(fingers licked)
I still admire the electric ethnic revolution of
the '60s
the temperature of the radiator
exceeds the circles of heat
remember when the eyes would speak
the whole soul
person ignoring eternity
with the clear gaze that haloes knowing

18

kill is almost a forgotten emotion
sacked
the tropistic car that poses the world
entombment in the nerves
needled
example: seismic surface figures
fissures in the wall (just the hand, writing)
or a total traverse — en route
or just to die upright facing
east into the earth
that motif
fate comes to see

19

fine art an idea list
intelligible for a language
an idiot doesn't have his own taste
a sex idea, considering the coma
the bonding reflection at heart
a deep need
of the intelligence to render one
perfect and rundown
sun no more comes in silence
naive, and tender

19.1

O Frank Stella so inscribed the light symmetry on dark terrific revolving really painlessly the sun in New Los Angeles Israel then interesting some stand (set) free of less than that than that the script sure of the surface especially Jill 1959.

20

a thousand spits
               brittled slantingly

_____

         but the offal
a death machine
of some kind

(paris sea the way out————————➤)

21

Returning & the journeys time wafted Olson's notes prairie
barnyard grain elevator pine siding mentality that hawk
circling within the head windows with a bead on eyes
(intense eyes) or fluid ears let's say cities mapped with too
much overlay keyed locked in his own handwriting saṃsāra
liturgy (I like west) you see saying it too near the sea you
know what I can't get over is the synaptic speed of now you
don't see it now you do make it up and it's not just all the
bodies all the fire all the love all this motion

22

Always think thinking inside myself no place without death
Kwakwa̱ka̱'wakw song sings or sit watch scramble and catch
last blue Pacific horizon no end to the complete thought
transference of which the words circled eyes Mao knew this
is the life writing questions even every rock etched in wonder
sometimes that song feels like the master paradigm or river
we return to with a sigh the archipelago syntagmed emptied
breathing but the body as a place that is as a container has
suddenness so the politics of dancing is a dead giveaway to
the poet's place is what takes place

23

Point with a stick better still a charred one that's it slots or
bumps to catch your foot or your breath forked branches
everywhere when we need them à la slingshots in the gulley
transphrastic symmetry sticks to the point I keep running into
this "soft pad of (the) feet" not as Mallarmé would say of
the hero *le talon nu* or it could be Bakhtin's jivey beak (de la
Cosa's eyes included) the prehended world on the contrary
dialogues the same but trees bucked and split or shadows
even that's what glaciers are and style is

24

The word "ancient" in your fire fragments through histology
filtered sememes with names deliver the mythology before
the first map of a cover-up brain-word always the flower
of creation black sun chrysanthemum at dawn on June 6,
1944 such "dragging the eyes" to the "eye of the dragon"
is no different from the notion of war as another temporal
relationship seeded I keep finding Yggdrasil from the
sky always beautiful and the Pleistocene cave cups East
European changed carriers hence the schema leaves all over
the ground and then it snows

25

Wall of the mind ocean continental trances inchoate rampart
wet cedar bark wickerwork *avec* traces whose primary
spatial finger "wants to live there" counterbalanced and I
spot you in the window with your lawless plan your *récit*
strapped with *ta'wīl* and bridge city as well the gentle sea
appears out of the table forever "waves breaking" the Proto-
Indo-European hedge in the Vancouver rain footsure in the
couloir mountains this is where the wall ends

26

Your own anthropology jumps like a bear from the apple
tree tonight her "breasts glistening" no foreign words there
except maybe love which comes after Earth as hunger
"tasting flesh in mouth" her depth anima logical triple
register reach for an imprint split between sight and thought
colour can do so it's eth as in ethic why any one returns
to the confluence plus edges of a genetic inscription or
homes another forgotten message carried there where the
character sticks and also the mother when Daphne insists on
the conscious I feel caught outside the tripartite red of the
apple biting the skin

26.1

```
that threads    in      S fold:
D facto         you     mythic yet:
her M           more    red fire:
next K          than    'membered SI:
line S2         y9ou    F edge
```

27

"one narrow world" in French is why signs in language carry
the secret imitation Kristeva points to in the hidden interior
polemic right here the "other" passes poetry as magic to
bury, chill, and fill our faces, hearts, and bodies the feelings
I have stand with Polo's journeying if a Pacific Rim could be
imaged up the liturgical sea and bells would have shown
the Khan some other Italian Cavalcanti or Calvino the room
of despair the sudden confusion runic grabbing of the right
hand to fill the left as you say "that might be anywhere"
that's what I think that flow is

28

Salt for the tongue's heart heartening desire paradoxical
cold and hot Canadian presence/absence mime's right
action right mind *et al* simple terms a vision Avison
teaches frames leaks hollows and flows in '63 she and
Olson walked out to the cliffs at Point Grey oceanward
falling west to "placeless place" he says she did not walk
out if you see his "West 6" but I remember the day and
it wasn't evening it was afternoon he says for him the
most important conversation and event was this Pacific
continental wedge "that marge / of the few feet make the
difference / between the West, and the Future" magnet in
the word finds this salt exciting if there was no wall there
wouldn't be the heat not just "Is" and "is not" come clear
as she says but how much "in the tongue's prison" of the
dream this overlaps "the rest is history"

29

Strip it clean the old scrub logography gesture for the body
to denote ideas so says the mythologem "in the middle
of wreckage" bare our selves for me it was marriage I fix
my life up each event is as hard to believe whole winters
on this hillside face west (actually a bit south) to denote
not thought or experience but synonymously such painted
over natural wood impossible Chinese Sam Perry helped to
get the walls and ceilings painted over everything it's still a
cave from where we dare to venture or love the word for
ocean doesn't stand for such a notion there are always these
planks over the windows and these rebuilt connections as
names "upon our breath"

30

Boomerang the truth in "How to Read a Map" or don't pay
attention to the terrain those signs that became questions for
the city the complicated tracks remain "a view of histories"
incredibly difficult shapes and languages but proportion gets
it together and south of here tomatoes still ripen that story
the mind traces feathers your hawk for example in motion
"counterbalanced by a movement a way back" look at them
they are not birds we still think they're stars or headless
moons that pictogram of "a closed universe" the circle a
story sometimes you tell yourself as Saussure says "covered
with patches cut from its own cloth" or that big boulder in
the middle of it "has an etching / a face" journeying and the
returns he called it cute

30.1

Jean and Jean Crotti and Degottex.
So what about the arrow "Explicatif …?"
and writing "time" by head and hand
but never behind with feathers or dreaming
as the sign art things touch it it's
just a fingerprint

31

Talking he said like a foreigner would get you snake-eyed
commentary or a tongue for booze in fact understand
cowboys and Indians as the ones to immolate because
that's supposed to be childish sensoryness thinking on the
horse or bicycle mind's eye world forever still carving the
bows and arrows from vine maple out of the gulley down
in Cottonwood Creek all running shoes at the mouth whip
stock for slather and the whole earth "noping" some image
of themselves one lifetime so Kiyooka says to Bowering
twinkle

(TIGHT WORLD, TIGHT LIFE. STREET.
CREEK. BARRETT BOYS' APPLE FIGHTS.
BALL GLOVES WARM FROM SUN.)

32

Patchy country for a mind slipped with willow whaddya
grow north of orchard country – dry, boy, real dry –
underneath thoughtlessness how history lingers as the blue
sky above Okanagan Lake on August afternoons below
eyelids drooped future furniture actually stand above the
farms and ridges of the Nicola Valley ever said he expresses
"hope" but the cool grotto of question asking almost infirmity
of the day, maybe money, I can't forget, no I can't sever
rather dissect event not sloppy vision (or even sleepy) shine
to squint at the intersection

(MEMORY AND THE DREAM
HALF CLOSED UNDER A NOON SUN
DRIVING WEST AT DUSK)

Indianapolis's European history is what you see in such gold
light if you look anywhere else place has always played
"country" and even this dude bought Johnny's apple story
and John A.'s fish. Same west, he thought, and that did
the implant for the journalist's tactile talk stories across the
country and into the side streets actually always on the
edges of the town are traces of the place prior to the white
man as well as underneath remembering water flows but
that's downtown kitty-corner from

(THE SCAR OF MY EYES
POLITICS AND RELIGION
NO APPLE TREES YET)

34

This synchronous surface of the page
(room of the city
the modernists still call it a building)
numbers and letter
names to which the human forms true
poetry visible
morphology occupied by thought
but still within the territory, all
and in the soil too, in
the soil, in the dirt,
supposed to grow

35

No, the words seep into a water table that connotes only
thirst and hydro, which is maybe why I'm uncomfortable with
the repetitive sedimentary taste-crossed politicos from the
movies and romance, at least if my life driving up the lake,
has something to do with it. Dissected lines like that trapped
in I want the image of warm wet snail shells vortical in the
gravel under three feet of snow the seasonality quivers too
much empathy with the hillside's membrane bleeding spring's
frozen wounded surfacing. Blind water, hidden mothers

36

I don't understand brute body and the institutions.
To exercise my faculty of synthesis, care for the new
    procedure w/ precision.
I wait for you and wait outside this occurrence of discourse.
The other authority here is the dailiness.
Certain people and others with names from the sea.
Alternate routes on the continent traverse the horizon.
Advance the impression there is an avalanche ahead.
Release all the other lakes, the glacier is no great illusion.
There are three dimensions that the body appropriates.
Memory of the search for the perfect formula.
Another voyage (the sky is like a fiery rose).
Observe you are not so obscure, but think of Italian

37

In her who is saved other than a lady of rumour
confounding confidence of a man
also a woman poor other than in the mind
mobility for a conception in language
the garment which exposes entire mental, la

38

In the dream the bear could be in the bush beside the path
and you wouldn't see him just the key and the tin cup down
where the log crosses the creek heart-shaped moss at the
intersection of the eternal event or when you get to the wall
will the bear still be with you just as she saw it such trauma
and trembling you're right is what makes the nation Cabot
Champlain Moodie Winnipeg but I want to know what on this
moonless night were you hollering and was there even a path

39

Fallacy she concocts with naming
whatever is the most delicious
(chocolate) moveable is
attentive to the other three letters
(I know, what three?)
small in relief, she waits for feeling
sees into the sun
Papillon (the movie)
and all the German rain which awaits it

39.1

encaustic "you"
literal vertical history
making French factory garments
your painting called *Slate*
imagine time made up
of materials besides "wood, various
papers, pins, powder
pigment, felt
pen, graphite,
india ink, mask-
ing tape,
plexiglass"

I believe you

but to not know thinking
whatever you called it
is never impossible so
the contemporary past "information"
so necessary to use stuff and other
wonder about it then
never name it, Irene

40

He says tatterdemalion reality and me I'm thinking body for
the ragged things now in the air all over the earth not just
America but definitely earth with roots dangling.

He has red all over him but he doesn't care even when he
dances on the stairs.

Lines like wire antennae, history, stones with secrets, stones
with dirt that clings.

Line-breath, points-blood, tooth-strong, hearted-light, bird-
early, headed-red, secret-god, music-mouth, felt-heart,
life-of-breath, precious.

41

Blake could see beyond places.

Cézanne sits troubled, yet he moves around picture-charged counter-parts.

Whitman marches.

Creeley.

41.1

Jack Wise/Christopher Smart
psycho-
      holograms
Giuseppe Tutti (is that
right?)

Whole earth all over
problem site sand
Blake going for no frame
full bleed

41.2

Blake's room along w/ Samuel Palmer's "visions
and models of the exquisitest pitch of intense poetry"
pitch,
    and dim light
    the morning stars
(Jane Shore's penance)
      "equal   paradise
      in all essential points"   keeps
                                      kindled

42

Is that the flesh made word
or is that the flesh-made word?

Is that get it entirely right
or is that somewhat wrongly?

Le mot juste or just tomatoes?

The poem as a field of carrots or stones?

You, squinting, as I tell you.

Telling you, you telling me, field waiting

43

Silence tells (talks), chant's attention, a good part of the truth
in sight of the unconscious, butterfly inside rock.

Whisper intelligentsia, murmurs Thoreau as an old Greek,
yet Pound (not Pond).

Rant these paper-thin words at paint or points, parts of
speech, gulp eye, ear, tongue, and heart to the heart.

As though vistas were car windows, pray for final blueprints,
middle-voice Olympic mounts, Oregon nights, twitters.

His poem, his rock, his home, his block.

Get around much anymore.

43.1

in words "these ..."
geese
amazing and subtle ...
pigments
of the period
    you walk on the stones of the earth
    each day of your life
    stone after stone

    water will not match
        this painted tissue or stainless steel
           feathers

   "Saera
Conversazione"

you know, regarding blush

and *pudeur*

rouge pad, our mother's
wings

all woman, Indiana's *Year*
of Meteors, 1961 earlier

forget to sing, forget the song
(*Chatham XI: Blue Yellow*)
    I have to know   all of this, like this
these
    subtle
talk song talk sign
       (ta dum)

44

All this wood lies dormant without breath, the shore Melville
saw but never mentioned, Lawrence in Oaxaca, Creeley
in Mallorca, minutely particularizing the mind, under the
sun, thought washes the beach but can't store the shapes
stomach does, memory, hunger, and love are the generous
chunks, this story is the same story about how landscape got
caught every time style imitates growth rings cylinder wall
scarred leaf mould

44.1

Nash's silent wood quarry diagrams lexicon of tree spread
bucked and split limbed sawn debarked and quartered
burnt piled dadoed spliced peeled screwed nailed kiln-
dried then baked bent laminated skidded thrown tripped
hugged buried finally old cedar tree felled in gulley voiced
in thimbleberry no dream no bear

45

He said it was made of stone.

Style, stick, car.

Japan, Massachusetts, or Bolinas.

There is this breastlessness.

Mud for guts. Now we know.

46

That's why the messenger has to make up the message from
yourself to yourself because the dream intercepts curiosity
as some kind of latter note on the design just to shore up
the sad story via the Milky Way or backlighting luminous
noumena mapped farther and carried as blood fonts flesh
first what an interlude

47

Under the skin right-handed poetry inside the car to work
out the modulation and correspondence of Marine Drive
lectures even on a Saturday morning he too looked out
from the subject side of his sentence not at the Straight but
middle-voice reflective the trees and the mist on Pt. Grey
shot out of 3 a.m. mornings of typing writ by ear and John
Donne's enchanted mind Robert Duncan's Portuguese
cape mad madder maddest Creeleyeye driving down by
Kerouac's riverside flowing peck peck peck at the teak table

48

Cuts two ways anything-America vehemence loosening
political world view literally for a world absolutely rhythmic
absolutely haystack.

Intermittent voice, intermittent silence, the whole man master
in stride and monument testing coastal continuity, checked
the metaphor Ernest F.

That dynamic of natural vowel just to get around the block.
No thing easy to be conscious of a solution; from itself hole
intelligence, open art open body.

Sound outside wisdom, gods, skyscrapers, countless ancient
world anecdotes drowns like a stone in a shallow pond
unless many ones make tense dust.

Rock of candour and abode of consciousness drift fixed
ideas to perimeter's eternity any Joe Blow relocks on that
landscape and that's not just too bad.

49

Butchered from the body.
No way to legislate.
Architectures I am.
Pilgrims, half out of love.
The possible figures.
Loyalties of the place.
Palpable, palpably –
Weather unmeasured song.

50

Going through the language of time.
Chronometrics. Horologicals. A book of years.

I like the water in it. And the footprints.
That movement. As you look for words
"*sans* intermission."

Of course it's the heart. Pictograph – pictogram.
Epigram – epigraph. Cardiogram. Histograph. The paw
again.

Cellular. *Un instant. Je vais voir si je la trouve dans ce livre.*

It's that "yelping pack of possibilities"
the hour as the order.

The predication, the pre-form of foot
in snow, log
on truck, finding out it never was lost,

                              fooling around

51

Everywhere I go here, here I go again.
But even if I worked it out ahead of time
I'd do it.

I know me. This train
crosses all the Chinese rivers in Canada.
Each one the same world water, the same
trestle, same deep gulley.

In Japan Mount Fuji no more
than a quiet, black Shinkansen tunnel,
out of sight, out of mind.

When Dorn said
the stranger in town
is the only one who knows
where he's been and where he's going
I could see Pocatello's tracks.

Your symbol as "accent
to the basic drum of consciousness" lurks.
St Am stutters and stumbles.
These rails are only half-continuous.

52

tongue mist lip boat brown gull hill town bed stone shadow
crow tooth rain boat flood hammer star gill shadow skin
hammer mouth town mist hill rock brown bed bird tongue
snow creek lip crow circle brown lip wave boat shadow city
light hill sky mouth talk snow gull hammer fog moon wet
grey stone boat bed mist skin gill word flood crow tongue
river mouth star brown lip night flood sail wave sky tooth
rock red bird shadow stone snow city blue hammer bed hill
crow tongue

53

God, how awfully large it is to sit here
lost on this log
without the im as you say from mortality.

But no *extremis* in this breeze for me. Things
such as this bark I cling to
deer chased by coyote.

Look, I don't want to appropriate his "words,
goddammit, words" or her "continent."

But I've lied, muse's
golden-mouthed righteousness.
I was where I was
but I didn't know where the others were.

These are muddy waters: the abandoned
messages released,
our daughters, chickadees already in January

54

How numbers make trails.
Track Li Po to Castlegar,
the Kootenay River flows down from the sky,
never returns.

Chance to get in the way
of water's predictability
or the white clouds of pacific
western mountain flesh.

Birth is like that, though.
Homes, mothers, names,
friends as images. Puffs
of imagic "rift or lake," anyplace.

Notation of these events quad right.
He's got ideas fixed.
Video la province, video la country, Winnipeg.

Hold it! When imprint hits grapheme
then eme is as in memory
                              just an echo.

55

Map of streets stream of dreams
map of creeks street of cream, fragments
and imago imprint, geomance a glyph,
a place on earth, under, or from it.

Name's broken letters maybe
words your body made.
Idiot bridges to parts of our selfs still lost
in the palindrome.

A found chain on the coffee table.
Some Scapes as a bookmark
to automobile between 3 and 6;
flex, flux, flooding, fl-

(ə Creekscape: Looking Upstream)

Fred Was. Fred War. Fred Wan. Fred Way.
Fred Wash. Fred Wag. Fred Roy. Fred What.

Creek water hits rock with hollow sound.

56

You look for the nutrition of yourself when you think of food
in this different way when yr alone, totally.

Does that "i" in "white explorers'" look like a sail on Lac des
Entouhonorons? Because of love?

Wounded, wounded. Parents and God, how hungry.

Hounded into the signifier ship, into the vessel, into
the mouth.

A big stone navel, under his feet, the cup holes.

Another god's daydream. The stage. Memory of your
voyage totally serious, a sixteen-foot oar, wooden
Wodin, Sutton Hoo.

56.1

Spots of blue dripping the "s" as a ship or at least
underwater and that not-so-little entrail of green like a ranch
boxed in fields of white blizzards square problems in an
active flux.

Or that "s" as some other kind of anchor outside this fuss.

Like that.
That little charcoal field up north and the Ace, 1962 R. Kitaj
not.

57

Just to think of the couloir colander the "m" is impossible
wickerwork boat of water music.

Weather on the sea only the deep soul empties out shining
like a village no wonder then the vivid river.

Not so much a fence as a fish weir (sometime giggle mesh)
never to be totally contained in fact you should've been a
sailor.

I want all that flood to be soft underbelly felt from birth to
be the message home and

That inchoate body we all lumber under the maw of isn't that
still the Galilean galaxy and all the little stars and fishes

57.1

the idea, Henri
moves

Mouvements, 1950 in sumi sign
tachism repeats

seeing
saying

appearances and agitations
not just the rock of ages
mind, too, splashes
expression all over

that mescal uneasiness
quivers

why study medicine
yet become a sailor
suddenly 1922 "art"
and February '83
into the Seibu in Ikebukuro

they know, they know
you have a hint of something
dirt
at the surface you thought
to whisper
a little gossip

58

Wasn't she Phoneme's sister? Did she ever learn to drive a car? Some said she was a beauty. Did you ever hear that?

That's a good idea. Write it all down in case you get a memory disease. We all do. Time is impossible except literal. Faces maybe. Sisters.

That little { really translates tripartite for me. And when I try to feminize the model, eyes haze into wheat and flat roads.

True geography? When Kroetsch arrived from Plunkett in his Honda I knew this place was all afternoon business. Excited but didn't mention her.

When Olson read "the genetic is Ma the morphic is Pa" what I heard was "paw" as in print. Maybe that's how Grammar gets to be the Granny

59

Around here I'd like to be
St Mountain Station
on the Great Northern tracks
in the natural situation.

Don't you talk of speaking singing
soul carried forward,
lines of a life, truth written
in the lie of the word?

Maps through the days make a lot of sense.
Imagine friends beyond these times
sure recompense.

When St Orm runs the alpine ridges
on Kootenay Lake,
on the beach, at my feet
single waves of history break.

Now I know the names to measure
in this language stream:
whatever rhymes with no sense
keys the dream.

60

Maybe that was saṃsāra near Abbotsford once but when
I was a kid it was Fort Langley and the train to Vancouver
Upanishads sometimes still when I drive by Sumas and the
U.S. border Fraser Valley cowherds now I smell the pig shit
when we hit Chilliwack I think often of that morning in the
snow all night coming back from Cid Corman and Seattle
w/ the one seat belt on yr old Ford around you and Glady
in the front seat smile as you hit the ditch didn't we roll
onto our side my side and George and Dave in the back
seat what the fuck and the drunk and the truck cop and
police station back roads all night snow storm finally dawn
whiteout detour sliding into yr folks home in Abbotsford
what a world we could have had Japan 'cept Corman had
Noh thing to say but that kind of driving got you India and
a narrative into the mysterious Dravidian guttural or as you
say in this story you rip up your own street

61

While I wait for news of the nest this possible subcontinental construct or model plugs the heat in the air.

It's those heats that stretch throughout our lives though, not the recent jet-age humid ones that clam our dying skin.

Especially the stretch that includes grandmothers as the walls of that ancient life we grow up in belief of.

Like the random notes you play in the hotel lobby, I think your view is a right full story, empty bullock cart, waiting.

Or Siva's rock phalloi excited in the world the Buddha stands next to, or that elephant "watching the bare earth self-fictionalize."

62

How did they stand as an exercise and how did they move
out of your way or did you touch when you walked through
the crowded doorways what was their breath like did it
make you think of a world breath under the sari how was
that did you find your eyes wound up in the saffron cloth
what if you had married a girl from Abbotsford would your
children have to leave the country is memory a horse or an
elephant and was it monkey play or monkey business in
the Garden of the Maids did you find any solid evidence
of transcendentalism in what way did Dal Lake resemble
Cultus Lake how often did you think of Victor Coleman when
you were there or Allen Ginsberg could I hear that egg
curry raga please perhaps with a cup of chai what's a Ghat
was the paralogical condition legitimized did you consider
becoming an orange-robed sannyasi and never coming
back? How would you relate this spiritual experience to a
life of therapy or crime

63

Art of Darkness tells poems about the great distances in our
lives revealed by doing numbers on ourselves especially
threes and sixes since it plays or shows it possible to between
the yaw of deep need and practice almost the result of stretch
and hunger for discipline such strict structure in the river of
ecstasy that drains the far interior watershed such feeding
of the nutrient ladder around which vertically unless you are
drowning swerves deep and heartfelt connections to not so
much darkness and light as some rather obvious waving to
the distant shore

63.1

Are those your rusted rocks along our shore?
Those lifelike mammals shallowed long
      and flaunting in green water
lolling bellies that fish fish-shine
      pure tapping thought smoothed out
sailors-take-warning morning?

Yet at that time of day flight becomes bothersome
since these are the returned over not so much land
      nor arctic eyes
      but the shining piss
of the philosopher's stone

                                    noctiluca

glowed last night, soft
just like the moss

64

The peripheral vision with half-closed eyes and the passing
cars.

The grid or graph and the brick houses along this street
in Toronto.

"The Mind of Pauline Brain" and a city, actually any place
come in and get lost.

The intestinal tract and the portable cassette tape recorder.

The weft the warp, the left the right.

The prison as you say the prism.

The word as an intentional flaw in an otherwise perfect
design and thought as superglue in an unworkable plastic.

64.1

Try seeing some March 4
quelques chutes de fabric

life and love (marriage)
her dress maybe

199 Lyndale Drive
                Dear Dave

it could be some kind of affixation
no joke but blueprint

even Toronto as an event
can get like that at five

65

Teleological mapping outside the realm of observation
architected to the brain the edge of which you get so close
to saxophoning the right gap this spark plug explosion
dieseling after the key's turned off invisible eme shapes
still hanging around when she says roulette to you what
is called meaning on the soundtrack translated two levels
under the lyric Hermes should have said not to steal from
yourself yourself

66

Split-screen concurrency like Williams-esque *Kora* repetition
to accommodate the known language conspiracy this
incendiary device shifts the fence out of the backyard and
into the melody with an equally careful telos to quote you
only then see F at that point does the genuine odour return

67

That old constant periplum positive/negative
        negative/positive
From Clarke's fingers plus/minus forward
        forward/backward
Or Prynne's North Atlantic magnetos
Channel one channel war
Something from the sun/moon exactly
        like creek from ice
End is the beginning and so forth
        that hated circuit
Locution gets to be locomotion
Old right/left mirror after all
Isn't really any message anyway
Just a jet shuttle on world's infinite horizon
Drive a cock-horse to Greenham Common
Cocks. Horses. Crosses.

68

A scatology of this book index back to front problem how to
reference shit sans number stone gland possible cold lump
in their throats after he spoke of his anus mucous faeces
foetus with a little warm piss dribbling down the leg who
is the little "i" who slid the bedpan under his ass with the
sadness of death looming large on Ontario's acidic horizon
whether or not it's him or he that's your anagogy for you
the middle section of *Panopticon* vacant of shit until the
repetitive fecal matter which writing blind bowel stirrings as
a narwhal from the body words that form the "hole" image
dogma mouthed unfortunately with disgust except language
stops to begin with

Place (by the water) book (a novel translation of another
larger) so Hesiod parodied somewhere place as a zero
something outside the walls like in I, Danny the King who
one serves or Queen not so feminist outpouring of the soul's
vivid mind (perhaps out of that idea of a "soul" I feel like
Buddha running from "consciousness") across the river from
here across the gutter is a support for language not unlike
Kiyooka in Japan yearly now space rented in an emptying
out of all the other spaces à la James Joyce going to get in
my mind all he needs to continue with or the voice people
from Québec Cedar map boat w/ motor on hearing and
the Delphi poem could be a bounce off the walls probably
a tying to the whole pictureness goes on between the two
moons woven at least tied up against the current fishing

70

"E" not quite there in Delphi's mind slope except for the
eggplant but on the *périphérique* the traffic is something else
not unlike the quick movement of the small bug attracted
to the light at the edges of the papers under the desk lamp.
Now it's raining, finally, after three weeks of heat. Moths
and what we call cedar bugs get in their last licks. Hermes
comes into the room as a stunned silence in the middle of
the yak-yak din, a borderline coyote too excited by the
lushness of the minutiae to pee on the post. This means
time and space don't really matter, viz. Canada, Cambodia,
Canaan, et al.

71

Called "fat bits" and it breaks up size into the labyrinth.
Goes inside the larger to really show the invisibility of
the city as only virtual; what remains are real streets and
buildings. According to Homer this change in the condition
of experience corresponds to Blake's beach. Heaven. Sand.
Could this be the shouldering of the world? The specific
seems to operate in this, as you say, abandoned way. But to
have daughters makes me wish, naturally, for the right kind of
jar, like the sack of winds Aeolus gave to Odysseus. Gingerly

72

Pausanias is the traveller but yr the journeyer and maybe
that's why you cry at night for love. Compadres of the open
road. Purest nakedness. Purest silence. Kerényi says "The
gorges over which [you might pass] can be the abysses of
unbelievable love affairs ..." Not to mention the deep valleys
carved out by the rapids of the Selemnos River, which these
days is avoided by even the tourists. Some path of sighing
and the sacred, some f-stop toward (or away from) memory.
Or did you forget you tied your sandals with a double knot

72 Addendum

Forgot nothing but remember the future when the owl's
hood will be cerulean and with a full tank your dog team
will break through those icy stars at the top of the stairs sky
deep and astonishing alongside the red Harley sacred to
Athena how the things have all added up packed in the boot
including that sentence you wrote in the dust on the police
car hood here the aperture is a pure drive along the river
in the moonlight [you might pass] simplicity the only bird's
eye of poetry step on it the high beam's still hoping you'll
remember the way home

73

Maybe the reverse is just the reflective ritualing of the prop,
old twin-twisted *kerykeion* to be leaned on. Any way think
of the Chinese dog days and how hot health can get under
this hound of heaven. Also, you'd probably get that mirror
effect walking up the hill straight from Pausanias's "scattered
Greece under Roman rule" simply because the Romans
omitted the phoneme schwa or diluted it. Thus the Socrates
ticket as a lasting embrace of those pine thickets on that
shapely walk up the hillside could only mean the sacred fork
or dish used to lift the lonely bull and later fish

74

But Hermes really didn't give a shit as the patron of lottery
looted the Apolline bank and simply rattled the mantic dice
not very apropos that lump of marble lint plopped there
on that hillside to convince us of the right answers to our
questions yet I've noticed how the wrong ones hang around
to stress the absolute equality of real unknowing the late
afternoon air and the dust settling onto Delphi's trees and
cafés stills the spring cool and refreshing to the tongue
thoughts seemed silent feathered and those birds (could
they be crows) overhead looked harmless in the light of such
hillsides now who can fall or get flung over the cliff for

75

Horizon full red w/ a few clouds across the sky down to the
river below Sentinel the dream gets dreary mist downstream
the dam gathers up huge hackles into the air these freezing
nights with the frost for the fog banks slunk against the
treeline each morning's memory of night travel and meeting
place in the ditch grass what voice Plato thought dangered
the elliptical island now that all this milk Simpson paddled
past simply for the payoff Fenollosa said wasn't there that's
what autumn is this year

Intent • bullet helps the daily postal cut through confusion
another language wing strut to world gauge reconstrue type
to lip which exits though body shuns the emic enterprise
in opposition a little minute particular on the surface of the
stone THE at the masthead even the winter bird hovers
beside the truth of itself in a dialect of heat almost fusion this
isness a nebula of a dense self-reflected frame that questions
limit so everything else north of especially not nation recovers
an afternoon life of its own writing through the punct

77

Earth seems comfortably familiar and sometimes strangely
familial so déjà vu green but when It becomes unfamiliar
or downtown centre decentral displaced place of all things
negative capability a positive incapacity to not know
knowing narrates not just Wordsworth's big something else
that is determines the rainbow of silence and noise with a
clear distortion at the edges of the supratactic acoustics
at one end and cosmology at the other underneath
dichten=condensare's ambiguous ochre dysfunction
fragmented rotten Rockies decidedly what's called fear of
the hatchtop or self-departure mountain arrived and derived
alter-native this making strange still oddly tied to wobbling
terra firma no matter what

78

Music here like the foot and door quick check of the imprint
assuring story construction and that unquestioning privilege
of narrative as knowing the only fiction seeming to be the
reader everything else counted for or lost only momentarily
in the cacophony of murmured concern that is itself distorted
by a comfortable pre-text almost uncannily like Cabeza de
Vaca's view of the new world old habits and all so scenario
is not so much a truth like metaphor but only the afterbirth
what happens later serves to trample the building debris
after treading the winepress alone entwined by the promise
of riddles and certain chronicles just for fun since the novel
is supposedly only a space project time'll have to launch the
rockets of textuary running the line so that a useful physics
gets applied to the physiology here literally heat and its
measurement but I don't mean the body's natural energeic
plot but more a form of ritual or what becomes speech
loaded and violent corresponding to such sad things as
Virgil's wolf in the fold and the anger of Amaryllis nothing of
which counts in the predicates of the ontology of anger even
this irritating gabble at the edge of the page book takes
over from the horizon not as a refusal of silence but then
not to neglect the echo either have you ever seen a space
not occupied by some sort of grammar the point here to
hyphen promise so that you recognize other events as more
immediate targets but that's prose for you always hanging
around to identify the self what a Québec poet calls these
eternal calculations that's what I want also the page running
and stars of intonation like swimming along the ladder since
anger has this prototype that includes retribution I'd suggest

cancelling the order and simply leaving the discontinuous
as mothers and fathers period being written like that isn't so
bad but even so imagine the possibility of literal language-
life a kind of narrative civilization that could tattoo for itself
itself and read only the past tense because in fact that's
the only hay to cut unless you'd rather consider picturing
someone else's lost garden I must admit I've thought of
everything as edible vibration for the pharynx and that's
one of those things you've got to judge prior to recollection
if the essential tools are borrowed off the bench how can
we mend our own soul or is this only frivolous ongoing law
as unself-conscious of denouement of the poor assaulted
reader of this facade used here simply to return you to
a resonance of recognition much like a boring Ontario
horizon replaces your attention with notions of elsewhere
so what are you going to do is fact fiction or are they both
strangers to music which is as much space as deep time by
the way sound articulates distances and fields and not only
pace to verify the solo variant of course to mobilize subject
do we need story but not as the cruelty of logic and the
ultimate "game" only to tell trace and the range of passions
that cause that inmost core to reverberate actually shake
the model up and kick past the door if we are right our map
has considerable light for the labyrinth my daughters are
the kind of immediate people I'm thinking of who would
never scoff a feast or possibly the goal isn't worth it a diction
moment usually brings new weather and all of us possess
a lot of randomness so why not confront this stuttering then
let the floods flash but first find out if gesture would work

and try not to let it signify ceremony but housework that
hum to the inner ear fragmented into short songs of plotless
therefore dreary life imitating a wandering or dreaming
mind whatever the mode ex out those long moments from
the future as if we knew why we chose any route but the
one home except to think we are already there the slowest
being the quickest though sometimes someone comes in with
news of the others this emotional torture gets to be a bit
vast if you let it take over as a mass synapse a little growing
awareness of stride will get the smack in the heterocellular
recovery that reverberates through the busy body from the
foot against a door to be kicked

79

Thought knot genetic still associational tripartite basic
relations as in microlinguistic BU BR and BS as Duncan
pointed out through HD Schrödinger grew crystal eyes
for the multiple yet maybe the whole chromosome fibre
an aperiodic solid this movement no net or labyrinth
Tisserande's body enclosed within the stars as clues that's
all we have this encyclopaediatic devotion to system
woven codes of straight desire not thread as a guaranteed
familiarity to pluck further prehension from the raven/magpie
bridge but as Jake says in *Feathers to Iron* not her epiphany
because it has moved on and you must do likewise simply to
keep up (with her)

Music at the Heart of Thinking
Eighty-Something

after Christine Stewart

I'd thought he'd riprapped that wall of the page or my mind
with mountains creeks trees and gravel years ago.

But then stone art pebbled the lichen with possible nouns.

Later story as an historical event cartooned itself; I played a
cloud of thought or talk.

Where to go to get the word rubble now or as you say fair
producing sky weather may eventually.

Music at the Heart of Thinking
Eighty-Something.1

Cracked surface times that the lake or seabed walked edge
and
     the path made reflective

stone
outside of romance let's embroider our mirror right to the
true
     optopotent body

Christine's holy city coned
Hyperbole's moving bull's eye

80

for Bill Sylvester

Yesterday in Chinatown I bought gai lan seeds. Chinese
broccoli. The green, crunchy stalks, blanched, and ladled
over with oyster sauce, make a fine lunch w/ rice, maybe
some barbecued duck. This morning in my daughter's kitchen
in Vancouver I think of you and the gai lan. The connection
isn't my choice; to me, your skin has always showed a flush,
a quizzical *pudeur*. Will thought forever credit jazz and the
exact measure of our fever? I think Duncan said

81

for Karl Siegler

Why then the one whirlpool when all the container
two leaks depth through its seams splendour
soaks the sands sprung three as song and not desire
for the polar axle gravity gave no chance for four
his meta(m) five outstripped his harrowing death
lyric left over from six both but let him –
us who want to be enduring messengers seven will
so said the wept-for fountain's Lament
only nine imagined water seeps from the mountainside
maybe that's why we wait or spring's beach butterfly's
touch informs new distances yet another story zinging
motive you and your bike's antennae spanned earth
but the words all over the edge thirteen taste comes
thirsty

82

for Bill Robertson

Sometimes all it is is a simple interpolation not so false from
the laws of narrative since you don't name her her perfumed
head imaged quickly adolescent freedom and all possibility
including everything to drink but maybe reading her she's
my girl this pursuit meant to include marriage as soon as
possible car job house who'd have thought smell could
linger in lingo or car tires whisper the light that night rain
right in front of all the happinesses prior to life and death
love's same old story could be that's when meaning starts

83

When I saw the angels movie
where we get to hear all that thinking out
loud speaking as Friday night theatre aire
(Writing more mass, maybe.)

Like that hyphen you arrow could be *saṃskāra*.
The dangers of the homalographic page as space
(could've been spice)
is that it might exclude the body
(The doctor puts needles in my back
and says I need to be faithful.)

Just think of the blur as flux, flax, bran.
You know, words
as white rice
not as good for you
as brown

84

Scree-Sure Dancing

•

home-truths pin-apples part fossil through fertilization flight
or eyesight could be sky or ducks fishing

•

recognize the plumes   of a Spanish   kind   of writing
ancestors   as certain types of Atlantic
animals   something from Anatolia   with an "im"!

•

History of the sky engenders the diverse faces of religion
All kinds of stuff like hooks and coat hangers inflate and
imprint there
                              Trace
                                (d)

•

War on your back
Raw no-words ruin
Real Clear Nuclear

•

"Ever try to copy Texas?
All those beans, all that plastic?"

– "I can hardly keep the road ploughed."

•

HERE WE EVENTUALLY THERE EVEN VELOCITY A
TIDE SUN (SQUINTING) SIPED PAST THE ART THE
SURREALISM OREGON JUST HELP YOURSELF CLEANUP
EGYPT AS A PLACE IN BRAZIL BUT NO FURTHER EAST
TIME AND RICE SEPTEMBER BURNT TEST TEST

•

thoughts different
sky's all animals, all
paper, all chalk. Our

•

writing as   the tableaus
anamorphous   =   of voyage
river cliffs   forgetting

•

She danced the strict linguistic sense
babbled *bavardage*   fingerpainted thick
memo-clouds in the darkening sky

•

h$_{om}$^{om}e

•

That's the secret
                    ticket
                              to silence
na [frame] na's notation

•

... each box of art jangles (*peut-être*)
a purchase on the edge of its own sequence
reflects adjacent body-language events even foreign
the container of white we unfortunately call history.

•

ohh   at nigh   night
Egypt
eh^x_____ap^{i}s_____apex

•

Maybe it was a dream grammar mountaining out the
hypostatic river as an approximate desire but instead
stretched striding or what I count on under the cedar tree
down by the road for final blueprints to the heart's property.

•

cellular memory linked to sunset effect
so *śūnyatā* revealed as absolute closure

•

I want one ethnic thing here,
right from the start. Dis-
orientation.

•

January birds
huddle on top of chimney
Wind the letter "A"

•

Loki, you
stomach

my sound.

•

Whenever I smell the raiments of message or caprice on you
I get jealous and reinvent old dance asterisks without code.*

*echoes

•

All the city
song, the great
city air.

85

Re a deer led to the lake only that fact self-conscious dare
who would say it again foraging for information behind this
hotel we don't think anything of it but re member that hunger
sometimes passes passion *avec* the memory of the very
night songs played *dromenon* with life's loves perhaps even
re collection as if that solved the wife and car syndrome
collated at some later point like in the bank or bag pre
played and reacted then drifted like continental tectons
across at most three or four generations to make family re
moon re sun settled self hunger honey just desserts

85.1

Mailbox + Letters Winter
Words + Terrace Out Tree mount No. 3 that
plus QNNET no meshwork. Domain
and Message Router Myfile {to} friend

the info texted invisible
lofts afloat w/ masks
image of the year as measure
'd logged out
bit scaped
more than just another marked ear framed

86

Exits and Entrances to Rushdie's Sentences

ONE. What if the phemic blasted page so what was once transparent appeared an eye-spot burning paper you know with the sun and a magnifying glass erasing words instead of antheming another spiritual mirage imaged fate as predictable as a butterfly's flight plan.

TWO. A scent of the fall sheer memory snow smells meltdown this Everest morph more aperiodic than widdershins and less likely resentment unioned by belief as a series of words than in the middle of juncture not standing like dawn hammers over the Himalayas but a flap-and-squawk V-line of geese.

THREE. If you could acquire a migrant invisibility in exchange for, like, sixty seconds, and that minute earth's contents recover moulting capability as well as faded anger with the presto of amoebean verses then walking forever instead of getting it back for nothing might turn the whiteout to remuda and you'd at least have hooves for tracks.

FOUR. Paratasein choice cut pickled and un knowing gravel to be one of the conditions of such motion slipp/ed from the pleasing though numbing eutaxia-tattooed sameness instead of.

FIVE. Is this an attempt to crack spin or a catalytic sugar made up to cotton the sweet uses of adversity with story's "then" planted in those spaces instead of poetry's timed gaze pivoted on possibility as opposed to prose's loss what is measure pointing at if not that quaquaversal heat mountained up and spooned as dancing.

SIX. The sign of the turn plowed back into place as this world wheel scoops out preaction in a twinkle circumcises heart such typhoon has no seersucker no milk no sugar.

SEVEN. If this renovation of memory turns out to be *dérimage* and we have to steer for the new world yet again in an *elenxis* of substitution then what now when the serial is only cinema and lists are needed before any action other than fishing which is best when it just *is* and not *for* anything.

EIGHT. Authority without text an illusion to master the distant and dissolving perimeter without search or government escaped containerism offers the tyranny of hot stuff contraband and never conquered without the fix or need for *dromenon* nor the hook.

NINE. What drew river to share earth neither overtaking the air was old scratch upon the world root radical that makes us taste like licorice unless you're white try ginger.

TEN. One reason why decimal was spotted on both sides of the centum/satem line was like the falling angel concurrently sighted with the same combination or polarity of surrender to the *hieros* but for the bird clouds interception of those tattooed letters rising from the city and maybe even this kind of patching of the rag.

ELEVEN. So there's this straight line to the question of hunger no way around the correct posturing of rule or guide me oh righteousness not to answer but middle voice got plugged with love-stutter that clot a wider need.

TWELVE. At first anguish squeezed news out of a hostile terminology for red yellow black and brown but pretty soon languages become mouths of painful non-tint jargon poking into the dream and then all of a sudden with snare drum crackling that heave of gut and protest untumbles the lock and *kapow!*

THIRTEEN. *Sans souci* the tongue hunts description until each morpheme gains kinaesthesis and then sharp motion pictures the memorable rousing as smoke or at least poked colour when smoked red.

FOURTEEN. Scope out the paragrams ahead and see if the divine isn't inhabited by some once-upon-a-time intention negotiable by a shh shh creeping up on curiosity as a kind of campground lure or kick-the-can espionage chance-cast into the emic abacus crying alley alley home free or any other text-spect (in-spect, re-spect, ex-pect).

FIFTEEN. After a while opinion becomes fierce burning and no longer dream has itself straight on how far from the cedar home is nor could nothing come only in pieces even though tainted such dexterity in the World Tree's branches takes hold and all you can do is shake violently these little boxes for books.

SIXTEEN. At least precious peace and the Friday sapphire are still pupa'd into the sanctuary of message where anima equals the last bark of joy.

86.1

Ahead art envelopes Beuys's *Four Blackboards* while
included in the width cubism narrated signage his word for it
"economics" arrows for HAPPINESS lazy reread

to shine fate determining futurism while a will selects dance

and away far away

87

The distinct noise clarity makes from uncondemned memory
beginning with small sheets of words turning very very
slowly slowing and knotting complete thoughts as sentences
or fat stray objects probably stories of writing's reality dogs
safely locked in waste land that far away from the perfect
just goes to show what writers take for instance Bowering
sans ing hopes for in a reader (confess it) mesmerized
biotext not history not space but fear runs weeping from the
imprint of fiction as a loaf of Triestian bread and all sorts of
alibis for making sense right

89

I've always had trouble with the ingenious engine as a suffix of graded wanting love or prayer especially kindergarten stifled kid as a kind of person who might extend racism or even keep me off the block your kindred jammed the oceans cognitive shot freeborn got then similar to most of the inborn tutelary spirits everywhere naive seed of Enyalion or old chip off the old rock and that's congenital heart buds gyna gendered and warped up tighter than a Persian rug how ginger's almost nicer than being born but that's just taste

90

On the weekend I got into anger talk about landscape and the hunger of narrative to eat answer or time but space works for me because place got to be more spiritual at least last felt now this water/genetic I suspect passions like anger suprafixed to simply dwells I mean contained as we speak of it believe me I'd like to find a new word-track for feeling but language and moment work out simply as simultaneous occurrences so I don't think you should blame words for time-lapse tropism e.g. ethics is probably something that surrounds you like your house it's where you live

91

Again only is it in the thing itself the place which is the
"driven" place as a warm motor song hums under the chakra
tree rock or stone creek song I've become used to such a
thing always drowning and then owning myself come to my
own self again possessed of me as the sib in the place of
itself hungry with love forgiven dreaming and knowing again
the tailbone of itself old bones claimed again so that "thing"
to my soul's bark floats again

92

Don't do anything
just sit still and feel the bridge above
forget about the traffic
    it's going as fast as it can
down here is the river property
    no train of words except some tropic text of truth about
old creek song flows its utter pure of coolness underneath
the fading rose another rose untangled knot a permafrost of
frozen words unflavoured dirt for roots
    all this leveraging aggregate compassed grounding
cord to compost loops the stomach's locomotor to Gaian
feedback shutdown more to do with stellar steering of
the junction box genetic or the freshwater hoofprint
of salmon salt

plane
reflection
echo
projection
cave
film
gauze
scat
entrail
residue
page
leaf
pile

book
descent
ocean
gaze
reprint
track
screen
tulle
actual

93

Any gravel road's OK by me or is that an ordering
intervention so long as it's not pure highway to the end
of the void without my story our narrative's just a bunch
of rotten windfalls under the apple tree of someone
else's eye a statistical cluster made up to cover up and
that stupid notion of a project as sticking it to everyone
else instead of girdling yourself to the entelecheic text
underfoot that dreamt you long ago

an earth doesn't add up to the only implicate map
ethnos is and

the new doesn't have to be the purity nation is at least
some love pictographed without lexicon gets us to the
repetition from

94

This is no mass synapse I'm after and I've known awhile
now being lost is as simple as sitting on a log but the fumble
jerked mystique clouds grabbing as the staked mistake
or stacked and treasured garbage belongs familiar to a
gardened world disturbed as heat

O soft anxiousness to be found again and again estranged
but marvelous then enlived slope of scree and marmot
whistle so that synchronous foreignicity rages in music I
want to put into a region of the cadence before falling's
recognized you know

where there's that disgraceful ensoulment Mao called
swimming

If he thinks it's a great privilege to fill halls and talk about
his own little heart when the invisible trunk of the noetic
is what's available on the other side of the wall and only
intuition can kiss the pebbly surface of Easter's stone just
as "it is not you who throw the dart when you throw it" then
could we not have called for a parallel play out of the
alphabet onto the red carpet of one's body through some
soul of potency no such dream of stars should floor us by
the raw and sober daylight of a cloudy sky

96

Repetition of the body as a means of carrying imprint.
Flowers, for example, couldn't get there any other way.

Looking at the ends first. Or that the digital eight hems.
Always prefer a circle route.

If this is the edge of of, that's skating. If those words aren't
full of an ankle then nobody'll read them.

Mountains. Absolute mountains.

One night when the moon was below the horizon the
one who had travelled farthest drew a grid on the beach.
Supper was over and she used fishbones to detail parts of
a bird. These were labelled p, u, and m. The kids sat on a
log labelled w. Some of us realized later that the moon had
gone under the lake and what rose above the ridge later
that night could have been larger and crisper.

Out of death.

Well, this summer it was limestone again. Acres of it. And
that's exciting because you could meander aimlessly. Not
quite; I mean a fragment seemingly a trail might reveal itself
and then maybe not.

Ten years from now I plan to stoke up the brush pile in the
morning. Some word will.

97

for Bob Creeley

Something stuck w/ no *dromena* until pre problema solved
the program of "forward" somehow the world you needled
me aged with words for such complex ingings of place
and person that vertical I-beam shot through the top of my
head in the Mexican café in Bernalillo (o crisp and drunken
mountain moonlit night) such pepper still not now never
silted out yet digging to remember such a world and any
other familiar thing, eh?

98

Pearagraphs for Roy Kiyooka

A collection of pomace. Left over. Residue. Pome poem.
Fruit, of looming backyard pear tree. Windowed lost love,
seasoned symmetry of gaze. Words to hang onto, picked,
plucked; pared, preserved. Or rain/frost-rotted brown on
top of the camper.

Nest. Branch and sky for hair. Dream space where the
eye-chaktra's rooted up prime before the mind's eye in
growth rings fluttered flowered house of interlimb, mesh of
mindingness, net work, nest work.

Some bright beam lights up behind the eyes, or through the
greenery, truths of all sorts writing pang and time. Tall is as
old is. That's a fact. Things to put a bite on, the bark. Getting
to the char-core heart with word-worm tunnelling. Put an ear
to.

Low roar of shakuhachi waves. Enki drumming on the cedar.
Hammered words said beep bent forgotten all but the ever-
resonating thud even the paper-clean dry seed-head split
and distant sound of frost released from brittle memory pod.

Old dogs of war words let loose as forkt birds slipping the private magic state into talking tree. Listen. Love words. Language paired and othered over the geographical heap, dangled from a canopy called earth-as-sky. Caw. Coo.

Facing the old yin-yang turbine round the night sky weaving its stars into the treetops shade upon shadow questioning distance upon distant sites sign voice weather noting exed ever only spins plus minus minus plus minimal.

After the throttle cutting of white inked into body along with the sigh of staining the world with the same body. What a river such tangible surfaces usher singing; its banks cut too with smells and other signs of shape or touch tuned with Meloids.

Word as seed preserve brings up the notion of rotten language composting for the progeneration of itself and the ripe vocable as soft and juicy palpable but for the bite of belief and the Bering Isthmus migration so far from the Cantonese pollen.

Chinatown walking through the food smelling and then sitting down in a booth to taste the bird's nest soup or any noodle late night neon ragtime all alone in the dawn music Virgil's vigil down the street and home again home again.

Stirred-up word leaves equal to birds' startled whoosh and
the morphophonic fruiting of the great vowel shift(s) syllable
canting the old prayer wheel so familiar as the resonating
fat of the adjective, you know, like "Summertime."

The tropisim of allowing the range of stimulation (in this case,
sky) and avoiding such an indicator as clarity of outline (that
is, fingering it) puts the poet's nose to the wind so that bite
has surface (in fall, that could mean frost).

Yes, there are a few of those brushes with sudden silence.
The "great" hush. A slight stunning of the uttering tongue
diverts to rainforest and you know OM is AM somewhere
on the Hermes dial. Even the trees wait, rooted.

Here the wickerwork of wonder prevails, especially
seasonal, especially winter. Night turns too. That's when the
griddle glows with answers, that's when the porch of stars or
clouds twigs to the forecast, that's when the eyes get used to
the dark.

This stoniness that comes to life, unfetters itself from heap
by song and the crazy clicking of the compass needle from
side to side, something ringing ahead, something diamond,
vertebraeic, maybe something bone-like in the name.

Sometimes it's just a light word as a reflective buoy nunning and canning entrance to the (h)arbour. At others, smell's left to gauge place, especially in the morning. The ode as a jar for dead fingernails. Pears, breathing through their skin.

Here's the tree traveller with news from the roots. For the poet that's the "heavenly" one, the one growing down from above. Not just the dream. The tune's reflective: the image of the tree shows a tree. Such is home and, underneath, the authority of love.

The tree-talk hears preaction (i.e., just thinking about it) as a plot to rejuvenate the locomotor birth-breath effect (you know, when the sap rises) because there always seems to be an un- or de- chat to simulate houseness.

Layered into west-coast leafery is another homing device between the legs for birds, rivers, salmon, spawning gravel, and smouldering midden heaps. All old-time warm, damp copulas charting ocean's peaks to get some home again.

Mother tongue tied lost ungendered gendering potent cone-seed to burst birth in any chance fire only words green branching into childhood pink Eve's apple stuck in man's throat all forest foreign but for the pear tree.

Behind this tree-braille on the slivered moon-pear of a page
is his "screech" and behind that some solitary hollering of
the pome poem as proper, as proprio, vessel for any world-
preserved jar of memory keeps listening for.

Tell-tale leaf-light filtered photosynthetic compost haunted by
the house syntax. Paper page so under the thinking thumb,
but then the word baggage tsunamis forth and tosses, say,
the persona of language's song which then just dangles and
spins.

Ancientness moving in on the dream of falling. Air
drama, into the earth. Leaf-word-paper-skin-mould, moist
churnowing of a tongue once flowered container of the
"well" sprung within body sapling dappled skylight seeded.

99

"s" love and South America not yet past her (larger now) foot,
bone, beak, star
beyond CBC oral – Swoop Safeway
    nebulae threw notions of panic this is – Cool

spring Paris
that's the wind through one of those piazzas
immigrate land knows sense the stick said water
                                       could turn
to snow – Exo/ekto
what's the dif since memory meant to carry over flake.

What I wants is a western Miss Am – Fascinated
by the spelling of Erika
left out of the deck work
rail watching out for the lean – Just like that
eye danced edge can smoke "the"
                          avec some ing.

Some poems name song and dream as an instrument with
which to pass by – Always a little distance calling over the
snow behind the trees to please observe the camerals.

99.1

Matisse yr such a disappointment today yr *esprit humain*
cannot save the boredom of a lifetime of nude prints money
and beauty even both banks like the jazz that comes out of
the mouth or yr flower letter to André Rouveyre otherwise
who cld believe now those're yr clichés'd prefigured Paris

100

Much white within bird.
North in August, that's their fall.

Light bends nice, in the mountains folds
each hill tucks late day.

Breath is the bridge all along, a winter sign.
Tongue's frozen words, air.

Then sigh said it again
remembered something.

Only the news hand tapped out of
shoulder a single white feather.

101

Text still as the lake this evening cantoed time late history
birded into the space nest the really real or as they say now
in Banff the virtual line gone fishing.

Song as wood chiming way past the rim shot further even
than any one instance of drumming and always outside the
sign parade even Jupiter aligns with Sunday school before
singing Star of.

Being led by words isn't so bad at least you can count on
them or they're like counting every time pebble registers
clear then there's the next leaf or ferry and if the distance
of the world doesn't work ignore the busy signal and dial
syllable AM herst 6-5740 talk about being led by the news.

Some plumed finger hot for some sun drawn into thicket
paradise's bird of reaching vision lands too close for
binoculars and suddenly years of cadence suck the
manufacture of duration into the middle distant voice so
there you see for you yourself

102

Line is a cut point to point
half of one world the other half
still available.

Anything but the next word
hold the present moment for as long as
you can hold your breath.

Anchors away with a sigh or me
caught with a double you too always fishing
hooked at the bottom of the bookshelf.

Heard enough of industrial hearts somebody
called him hammerhead and I thought
he'll never learn grammar too.

Book stripped tree to logos stump some
lumber caught scale and went to jail that truck of
interstellar logging events meant.

If they stacked us by our first names
we'd be at eye level Phyllis Fishstar half
truth at the Shinto Gate.

102.1

The Hands

> *très petit*
> but vociferous
>
> layers and layers lies
> noises born in Canada
>
> trees w/ meaning tight
> French sentences, played w/
>
> number
> a clarinet, a glass of sherry
>
> they yell meaninglessly Phyllis
> this birdlike looking, looking

103

On one side sigh hangs and through a window sand and
flowering vetch land's a floater or some simple blunt of
weight against balance only another frozen pea-bag to
shoulder mind *un poco, un poco* a turtle measure of memory
proprio'd slightly above and two feet behind your mouth
moving to intercept the note intended as Loki's cue to lift
song no repetitious paper-dragon Chinatown or any city for
self this rhetor caught in our maws had better be shaken or
taken Tiananmen

104

"Snap" for Hannike Buch

1   Some body parts of the move into the world
     show up as replacement parts
     Is there a finger or is there a tongue
     to be recognized later
     perhaps Is like walking
     cameraed through the European woods
     and peripheralled out to Paris *bois* by bus on Sundays
     lean gap as if creek stone or hand over mouth
     how do we watch for logs and other dendrita
     there curled (check weather report)
     layered along the banks so that part flows/makes sense

2   Fiction's window for example
     my neighbour and the prairie sun shifted
     single ridgepole into two tip-to-butt cedars
     who now knows what news when she opens the roof
     closer to paradise and strapped to her door each morning
     such fashion for today tests for sky's emptiness the figment
     and dance of any (finger) pigeonhole aperture

3   Tree the word
     becomes eye-pegged business *virtù*
     all Jack O'Lantern realism just a piece of cheesecake
     snap to lock title page careens out of tilt
     or should if the virago would just cry out the curious
     but doesn't this plastic sign need a playlist (doesn't need)
     either tight gut silence or stony story

4   To evanesce is possible
in just over two thousand feet
such separations today silk our covers to touch
just to mull over the marred surface of thought
glazed with snow — silhouette visible
no need to look up even breathe

5   Who told stomach how
as if to depend on sigh signing
enough to blight the plan-hole
now just try this one out OK
walk in on the true dark
that same blue park
no catastrophe but only so many nights ever

6   Straight 4/4 time but just a little
clouded over the ridges
just a little eye in the sky little riff for the skiff
even what gaze set off toward first rock
until hackled in white somehow 'istory
all our farm clocks telling
get that package to the edge of the river
where it waits for the pickup while out on the bridge
how does the page gel root at the same time how does
the double tongue ripple the noon day pond

7   An assumed name and voice thinking
hum can look so scared shitless with edges
is that a problem the north follows around
meanwhile period
pencil finger thumb rubbers the 'istory of the book
and post-place
is that the point or dipper of the American drum
or is that coke

8   A quick blink
but just because the first page turned quiet
doesn't mean we'll forget
in fact nothing cellular about time
the supper bell'll ring
whenever belling's needed

9   Sometimes leaning shows
but after that architecture churches
a picture of the perfect ridgepole as a nautilus transit
mere yawing on the backside of the moon
saved as virtual in the promise of belief
only one before belief two
then how did she know it was all
tight ripple-grain around the knot now a ladder

10 No secret tidal
dialogue moving in
on the almost
open Persian Gulf
from under such
cradled rhythms
anima hemmed in
by all eight mountains
counting

11 Being born grammatically correct
isn't technically season
just wordless options for genre
until good luck's red paper peeled greeting
severed scrap sewage new year's
year of the yet named
time starts tale varooming page
to spine page to spin

12 gut cut
but touch
still stirs
slight all-American gung
straight-arrow sign
language plays
in the cards

13   Unthawed tongue
talk talk talk
telling the wind names
found in foreign currents
the sound of quivering rudder
biblio'd at the heels
but just local
locally twisted

14   Then what kind of pattern can you back into when lake
and river surface eclipse in that diagonal sparrow of global
day-to-night which becomes then the other story known as
the Norwegian surface until someone from inside Québec
quizzes how deep's the paper in that official manner meant
to determine bona fide spic-and-span krino-sift

15   How to get the lyric to emerge
where the paraph boils
is that the purpose
of the combing process *volte-face*
of a tripartite world's stiff calibration
of enlisted tactics to get home or even around town
but to arrive at the stem of a new world all portrait
or how else undice the lustre of the line

16   From late afternoon almost to dusk by the time they get
maybe seven nibbles at America and then
Art formatting rosy-fingered paradise when who else but
animus tries on the Massachusetts slaver forgetting that the
hook was baited in favour of hunger even though they've
practised can you tell the chubby cooks their reputation's not
left untouched

17   Is it really because the moon was tied to the pilings
with maybe five or six gamblers suggesting the next move
just because the lake we live on is a dog-leg lake
or did she strike out within earshot of the tin drum
chimes hazarding what old cliché on virtue
from the glossary of voices in novels and valleys basket
if so
then how can we believe the fiction of trips
will deter the determined nextness of story

18   What good is it
if her ears heard gut
how lucky his rabbit
didn't doubt eyes
like periwinkle knives
or the binnacle housed rowboats
(and that was Belief One)
from earlier days deep
into the night

Noah couldn't think in words
except to mutter grammar plus,
that asphalt tongue had to be a tenor
so what good is it to involve artifice
just to come up with something

19   Certainly up around Leduc
Alberta pressure-treated virgin duck
there before straight bushwhacking made maps literal
gills is what gets us up the hill of the genitive
appendix but breeched birth's anger no euphoria
no end of any story gingerly born
just more sons who can work
the final name shift but each daughter stuck
with a tongue to taste the frozen rail

20   Some granite over her shoulder
into the wind, Toronto
balmy, almost sun through the haze.

This is her Mediterranean eye:
crushed stone cement lampposts
stained with rust from the bolts.

Sneaks a quick flash of wood at home
determined to double her mirror

21   What annex of names for northern Europe
not calendered
under a tripod of blackened driftwood
totemed upright on the beach
could guttural the night without blur
and craving infiltrate charcoal gone
wild for alibi

22   Is this ladder to decline the yoni
or to invert the horns of the ziggurat
to the clit of desiring night.

Whatever kind names
jazz at the Palladium,
same cross. No noodles.
Just steam our fish in black bean sauce
and something bitter.
Or why the main character
has a nose to job.

23   How if why pirate the genre ship
when you can try stamping the body
with the flood of forty-eight
back then it was no secret
we would all share the same formula
for invisibility intended to clock (snow.)
(quells.) (sameness.) (time.)
and time again

24   To say says mouth
words story spicy news
or siping the Green Door
for Shanghai noodles
she says they said pretend
but snuff with Hermes's stealth
no need to filter the action
why not atmosphere this form tonight
right under your nose
back into the menu

25   At the Wildlife Centre is a "Turtle Crossing" sign
that the body story follows earth
that's what we could learn then
what the wall of sensation nurses
to avoid but revere the key
and then what the hand seeds,
all cards to guide the next bluff romance

26   Shouldn't we begin with the sort out and deliver task
since that sets the pulse
and whatever the Sirs say
don't stop at the border to mime fragment
every true aesthetic rifles her lied on Saturdays
those're those purple afternoons

27   Some of these feathers washed up
draw out the local what.
Could that be science's sack of the positive?
So stomp!

28   You can have a side-to-side door
a side door
a door that opens and closes
and if you want a door that disappears
then you'll get a real name allergy
but if you get tired of the code of theory
especially those cute rectified arts like the novel
plus the one that goes up and down
the one with stomach cramps

29 What comes with all that temporal morphology
that endless propagation of the sub-father
that belt the son is left to shine
no sharp, no axe needed
for re-reading the rough opening
and now will animalism handle that hatch
to blaze our spin right outta there

30 Isn't how she could plan keeping
dependent on Plato's spread
if the transitive purposing plot
comes all the way around
to repeat the solar stamp
you know, gets too singular
and repetitive almost plate-like
these charts of government

31 Maybe we could strip
this ponderous ark of size
and sniff page
right into the gutter
with the numbers
seeing as how humming's
flood's filled
no wash no meaning
but very clean no punctuation

32   nine
nin
nie
the three *belles-lettres*

33   No clear-cut logging on this property
if you think of the margin as a wing
how would you not contain story
or think of a menu of alignment
accidenting itself on the driver's side

34   No
not a sigh in site
nor could "i" find
design in singing

35   Housing always knows
we find out even
when we only understand
the lie

104.1

What with the air or brick and you open wide in the blue
intense blue sweater electromagnetic field coordinates of
the entire swoop run north/south tumblers interlocked at
the code post-elastic in case anybody gets to you about
your cheeks sit in that blue waiting all over the background
your mind world beyond the wall even the dress you wear
mapped Dutch desire

105

Si Sismal

si aboyer ou noyer la voix
parmi les images et les mots
éveille un peu de crainte
abrite alors la figure choisie
le bord renversé de vivre
labelle spacieux

si quelque tissue de soie persiste
sur les lèvres et trop excite
respire d'un air naturel
même si demain va vite
dans l'anatomie
cherche d'autres récits

si à petits coups de langue
d'expressions la tension continue
rapproche les mots crus
l'horizon s'il le faut
jusqu'en la bouche

si le timbre de la voix
se transforme et que trop de chaos
ou que mélancolie s'installe
combine la variété des réponses
la théâtralité de parler

"If Yes, Seismal"

if above barking or knowing
noise the voice farms images and
words for life a little crazy we
think but all right before the actual
figures choose choice the border
labels space in you

if any tissue of soil persists here
on the heart much too excited
could be the air's too thin
naturally some same body
remembers too late
to search for other recipes

if a small cup of language
soups intention with a continued
expression against word crust
until the horizon of approach
whose fault whose lips

if the forest of the voice
transforms into the trope of chaos
or melancholy installs itself
in the parlour of surprise plant
variety re-speak pond

si ça recommence et qu'il fait
   chaud
trop chaud encore dans les
   jointures
appuie partout sur le quotidien
il reste de grands trous
des saveurs inexplicables
baies, corail, littorines

si, tu trembles, tu vois bien
forcément il y a du blanc
c'est vrai et forcément
tu trembles

—Nicole Brossard
   from À *tout regard*

if the see-saw bounces back
   hot to trot
trembling shows up again
   late cell
synapse applied part out on
a day of rest great truth
a vague smack of the lips
baits, coral, littoral

if yes, you shiver, you see good
inevitably there is some white
it is true and of course
you tremble

—trans from Nicole Brossard's
   "Si Sismal"

106

Wasn't that Arrow's error eating into the wrong mind a few
more of those *rhythmic* days that *just don't seem the same*
these days of uncanny sublime biology but linger in the
haze of transition *'scuse me* while the nomads of *mental
practice* check both ways for the washed-out junction where
not only the topsoil is lost the gravel the culvert the whole
goddamned fold has disappeared though not the Going-
to-the-Sun Road built for the tourists of *unified mankind*
who drive by and ignore the chorus of "Help me, help me!"
singing from the trees *'scuse me while I kiss the sky*

107

Now here's the cultural kitchen *dîner en famille* complicit
with what's for supper that moveable feast yet no nomad in
our house just soy sauce salty (rice a given) when I stare into
the wok I bark into that mirror steamed with invisibility and
splattered with black bean sauce, fast food Freddy, you'll
have to check out before they'll know you were there, no
curse of plurality on my unclouded skin just the burning rays
of a half-bred exit from whose gaze

108

Loose Change

Now I know I have a heart because it's broken but should I
fix it now to keep it strokin' or should I hear each piece as it
is spoken and stoke heart's heat so hot I smell it smokin' or
could this clock made up of parts be jokin' that missing spark
a misread gap provokin' and little sock of baby breath not
chokin' the piggy bank of words much more than tokens not
just the gossip love is always cloaked in nor all the meaning
text is usually soaked in but roast potatoes for a tender
button so much depends upon the things unspoken and if
the heart is just this clock around which clusters all that's not
and if the of and to an in that it is I for be was as can set
these el em en t's far apart please hasten slowly old tin man
I'll stop right now and have an egg because I know its yolks
inside and what I have to do is crack it open

109

like a lit match to straw

like an easy catch to a girl

like a cross word to a tree

like a stuffed bird to gravy

like a crow's tail to a square root

like a bent nail underfoot

like an old shirt on the job

like a folded yurt after war

like the crumpled horn in a bivouac

like a Kansas storm in a plot

like two old potatoes with dirt in their eyes

like a few bold credos on a tattooed arm

like the rhyme in brain at the end of the train

110

Under the shade of an alibi this land haunts its thought with
voice the word repeats (though thinking can't) the shadow
of a broken Kachina doll one ear lost to the yellow of the
dandelion, green wants to return this Pueblo in exchange
for an icefield, so now who's frightened by the ghosts of
repetition, the level of the lake inside history, that's the spirit

111

The purity of spelling nests in the bole of a cottonwood
tree out of the way of those muskoxen syllables in the
distance with their potent loads on their backs each letter a
nameless squirrel all eyes and spasm chittering deep in the
encephalitic roof gutters looking for an acorn of truth that
might last through the winter

112

Citation that close is a way to deflect being full of yourself
or if it's the history of everything then an epigraph to our
century could be some big *"voice lost from the person it did
belong to"* suddenly stopped, look, listen, then follow the
emptiness around a big tree nearby just to get out beyond
the last street, the city limits, anyplace, anywhere, but get
lost, just like Christ's strawberries, so to be not full is to be
full or at least nearby

113

The signature in parenthesis *sans souci*
the body of authority contained for shipping
(with string attached)
for example local movements could include
Lake Frank O'Hara fossilized or broken Frank Slide
better not call it politics
but keep an eye on Turtle Mountain's sliding signifier
sidelined for the moment yet repeatedly
folding fault until touched into action
mind winding down the list, ah!
there the fine(d) nature of bodily sensation
being carried on your shoulders is pretty good

114

That's the drawer of poetry, closed to keep the lake from flooding. *probably the secret of syntax itself.* Indefinite junktures of the hyphenated -eme-clutter posing in wait for a synapse or quilt of meaning. Nothing's wrong, in other words. *a humming sound, of bees perhaps.* Just throw it into the drawer (*twisted threads*); mess is poetry's mass

115

it nothing does to holler
there are and it is outside this

it nothing does arguing crows
instead of to distance oneself behind this
that's a cal lamb of tea
         Opal might say, "the near
         is too close" – which is
         her feels

Lars Porsena flies to the top of an old fir
Whiteley whispers, "Bring it all closer
together"
he caws, "Truth gives no news,"
then swoops into a black signature,
"meet me in Albion,"
since distance is presence

115.1

Outside Emily Carr's lone piss-fir these throats that are long
in art and free-standing poems wall the provinces no more
rail yelling every spike a chink

116

Postpone the ladder but remember to discuss the number
of steps since they are but mounds swimming up against
the particles which deflect into the cant of shore the
ultraviolet climate, the lean-to for the potential snowstorm,
falling for the tilted edge of bed, the clinic of the night and
disappearing weak spot of forgetfulness's "why" the poem
lists north or stars fell on slopes

117

As Roy K. drives west across the Burrard Street Bridge he
sees the harvest moon rising over the armoury, balanced
huge and bulbous along the top edge of the Molson
clock. The two Os in M_LS_N are burned out. "I feel the
cutting edge," Roy hints, "of an un named neon stalking my
vernacular." The Owl of his glasses blinks and he chortles his
"haw!" at the magic of the night

117.1

Marian Dennis Running Arms
Susan Penner Curly Hair
Bald-like Sleigh Machine
Pyramid Wheeler Outstretched Seattle

Moon

flight crayon pink plywood backing
for Christmas *une guerre civile* 1971
memory embraces on the lawn chair
her legs (Susan's?) disappear 1977 1987
whistling

118

That mouth watering along the breathing surface of the lake swims home, her wake an answer to the shoreline.

That time the smooth cedar deck whispered feet, her afternoon, the count of lap on the beach stones five after five.

That huckleberry patch is Pauline's secret white wheat, her *katha*, the answer that is the question.

cat's cradle

For myself, I realize the cradle is where I want to be.
Despite the threat – and this is central to the torque of
infancy – to erase temporal discriminations of difference,
I desire the potency of training, the buzz of the tracks
under the wire, the fusion of this fission, the unsettled and
dissonant noise outside the hypocrisy of permanence and
purity. The community of the cradle is, for me, not a lonely
place to be. As I said, the homogeneous insistence of the
continuous string will not contain my cradleness simply to
define its own obsessions for clarity and univocal meaning,
i.e., its tyrannical demand for symmetry. Patterning is
multiple and I've discovered, through the elimination of
the ladder, this rejection of paradigmatic experience by
the young (but not only the young: "urban Indians," Asian
tourists, skinheads, and family breadwinners alike are
affiliated) a kind of coalition of free-floaters, those of us who
wish to cross over on the opposite side once in a while. And
we are not like those cartoon characters of our childhood
who can walk on thin air as long as they don't notice it;
falling is necessary for dexterity. Both infancy and history
have insisted, through the hierarchies of a knotted string, on
the dynamics of improvisation – very simply, how to fake
it, how to make it up. Allies in this configuration of the gap
have been artists, carpenters, and fishermen – both taut and
loose – who, for their own reasons, have also occupied this
disturbed and disturbing site. Through a substantial psychic
reality of desiring objects, I long ago felt the need to contest

my so-called "mother cord" – its dominance, authority, power. Another important ally in disturbing the normal tightening of the reins – a sometimes disposable reflex between two intentions, pure ones at that – has been the discourse of the chalk line, a volatile and stained venue that in the last thirty years has challenged how its productive agency has only been granted, according to our neighbour Bob, through an act of colonial line-snapping. But what's certain in this rope-a-dope debate is that you can't always get it just right. The desire for the perfect simply produces another object, a *fait accompli*, the repetitive delirium of rusted strands of wire cable, the invisible knot in a piece of sewing thread, the tattered and exploded end of a shoelace, a cauterized umbilical cord. This is not at all a polarization. We see that the ligament, like transcendental silk, is what remains of the tension when, at the end of a long haul, it is stripped of all its strength and fibre. The nexus of this spiritual experience of the line as a trace of thought has been recited by a Persian mystic: "the string is the string, nothing else; the string is the string, all of it ... the string is the pure subject of the verb." This framing of the cradle does not mean that you can't read it. The sub-muscularization of the braid can be interpreted as caught within the progressive dynamic of Tourette's syndrome where motion and action by a sort of sensorimotor mimicry involves, in the words of Giorgio Agamben, "a staggering proliferation of tics, involuntary spasms and mannerisms that can be defined only as a generalized catastrophe of the gestural sphere."* This string is no cyborgian extension of the body. It is itself, its own nervous system allowed to

---

*   *Infancy and History: The Destruction of Experience*, trans. Liz Heron (London: Verso, 1993), 136.

talk back through the permutations of an ever-transmorphic screen saver. Metaphor is not easy to come by in describing this locus: binding twine, floss, packthread, leader, hamstring, lace, and so forth. Caught in the velcro. Catgut is tempting as a forceful interpellation. But who will answer? We can find no spider's ethic here. What is held by the two hands is not meant to measure, particularly the fingers. I think we need to get wounded, down to the nemo-fibres, the ciliolum, the yarn, the thong, the rigging, the ribbon, the bandage. Yes, the wound. The interstitial space of a stage, a balcony, the trace, finally, of a scar that has borrowed its outline from an imprint of the domestic. This is a track, for me, not to the realm of the spiritual (what an illusion) but to an inheritance heretofore stifled by the intentions of sacred or economic models. I want to be free to use the crumbs and scraps for the crumbness and scrapness in them, for nothing else. Time is, etymologically, according to Heraclitus, "a child playing dice." If this is true, that is, if this is true for the cat's cradle (and mine), that string is a yoke to the spinal marrow, to the breath, to the body and its threaded thought. I want to be there in the heat of their trans-, crossing, why not, through the residue of meaning Métis many midst mingle miscegenate mangle magma mongrel mélange mess melt me ...

120

came to the place of thinking
found along the shore of the lake
submerged maps, heart-clock
diaphragmed into two pears of iron filings
rock terra surfacing the prevailing thorn
pith such deep purple, not chinoiserie
but gene pool highways and mountain ranges
Drum's edge of of
the old bearded lapis man, hunched miniature
reappearing through the mist, tea house cartographer's
green jade route
could it lock origin?

when you push against another's gods
doesn't it set up junctions? missing engines
a half-breed, that has possibility, even beauty
a ringing at the door of the poem,
floor tilting door frame unplumbed, mitre missed, never a
road not taken
demystification's new mystery further studies
the day as the place

brief to Butterick 7/29/88: unless cut
this vetch will dry up and go to seed
Calypso Lille   Frank Slide Harebell
Clematis Creek Humming   Proof of the Crocus,
Idaho's the panhandle she said
Za'atar for my bread and cheese
driving north of the Bitter Root

conscious it's a secondary road
and darker green this valley

have TV breath   old boy piss   retiring to his
Connecticut pasture
some alumnus to be the rector of poetry
to play some tennis, so said Rodefer, slipping
today it'll be over thirty the Scotch broom still yellow

Thel's Eagle asks the Mole "what is in the pit?"
the root within the secret air of fading?
Lily of the Valley, Cloud, Clod of Clay, and Worm?

Dying means dead.
Move along.

121

Strangles[*]

1   Why return dispersal's genetic wanting one ethnic thing to
show itself in the breakup of a marked body to keep out
of sight of the package to trip the diapause of meaning
cut the key into accent unexpected tumblers open to the
many-forgotten messages hungry for new arrangements
punctuated forever by those silent triangles of breath, just
that, breathing

2   If the surface of the page is really synchronous with activity
then the true morphology of alterity, "the cedar-head that
needs the cedar-feet," the round and the square, the feathers
the iron the crack the stone, the name still occupied by
thought territory, syntax of the re-, routing and writing, all to
make poetry visible, to right "the lightning flash that connects
heaven and earth" off of its habitual lodestone, not just
flip the magnets "four steps; negative/positive (forward) &
negative/positive (backward), or no-yes/no-yes" but still some
emic vessel that narrates the dialogue home, water, egg

3   Some critical digit stutter of knowing both entrance and exit
and that same trestle same deep canyon of syllable tunnel
coming through strapped to mind dubbed image a hail
of intonation that moment's Chinese river nation zero still
packed with caboodle these signals putting in deep time
pause fast forward rewind

---

[*]   Written as "chimes" for my collection of essays *Faking It: Poetics and Hybridity*,
edited by Smaro Kamboureli (Edmonton, AB: Newest Press, 2000).

4   Say "Sheh!" to get up from the log to get lost and put into
cadence the synchronous foreignicity of zone in order to
track your own ladder of leaving swim into the next story
some starving elephant as the imperial slacking of alterity
just such a gap in trans to collate the *terra* of potency
except for being frightened by hunting this dispersal of
planned punctuation will rob the arrow of its feather the
dart of its you

This is the juncture of the moment that requires action, needs
to be voiced, even though one might fear a shift from the
quiet sitting position to the forces of navigation and their
necessary paradigms of anticipation, estimation, and trial.
The synchrony of estrangement, the unknown, and mapping
could be as simple as climb that ladder, learn how to swim.
This is, of course, a privileged style of movement and can
be seen as a gridlock that excludes the external, starves
the senses. Wherever potential openings can be located,
intention is reminded of its uncertainty and at the same time
gains new guidance systems

5   Recognize cousins as those sub-paths of relationship just
happening upstream

but try to turn that feast into the trace of a biotext that isn't a
net or even next September

distinct and personal some kind of syncopation of
chronology that bumps heart into the hyphen of chaos

no theory or category in these narrows will catch fish

so what if they get away the critical distance cut by
everybody dancing like crazy, eh?

6   fragment is such a city that might shake the lingo up and in
the simulacrum of an earlier Vancouver kick past some door
on Hastings as if it were the On Lok on a Sunday afternoon
so we might be right during those wet, grey seasons some
European intermezzo on Robson silencing Cambodia
and John A.'s map with its considerable anguish for the
approaching labyrinth after they tear down the viaducts our
poor daughters are on the immediate frontier of the subject
I'm thinking of they would never scoff a feast or possibly the
goal isn't worth it diction and dictation usually bring new
weather

7   No mass is without something else, something added, other.
The one and the many. Taste a gradation of foreignicity:
we came across some abandoned specific with the
realization that it wasn't represented in the sphere of
culture surrounding us. These particles of recognition and
desire, subalterns and alternatives, solids that could melt
into air, are what we use to intervent and domesticate those
aggregates of institution and industry that surround us

The shoulders of eating, the sack full of ginger, the Blakean
beach, the word at the end of the word, the curl from
kulchur, the grade for the course, the genome in their home,
the rap at the door, the spoon full of rice, the chop for the
lick, the tongue in a knot, the circuits of surplus, the milk on
the way, the time of the day, the water over or under the
bridge, the other side of the tracks

8   This is it, the orifice of memory, a little Zen-hole of meaning floating, the fissure in the last world where the fish come to die and the navel of truth a ziggurat of erection and clitoral inversion beyond dying that ancient fold reassembled in as deep and dark a well on the other side of the wormhole of grand systems some sudden chatter of the body to replace the silicon of purity with feathers

Some things get through and when they do we see the opening. It'll close quickly enough but for a brief moment the world floats in replacement mode and in a passageway the rift between an ordered body and a musical body is seemingly healed. That amalgamation is in a continuum where the foreign is located

121.1

So sad 1920 Beckmann *Carnival*
could've magnetized this place
this page cld.

122

First you put the puck into the net
Blind and intended
old-growth free
         timed
All for the of
         equanimous

Game on: disengage
or share the blind spot,
all that me-ness, inside ...
blindsided. She (He)

         (Notice how the pronoun gets evaded/
avoided as a kind of cultural punctuation in the hopes that
"family" history will become "class" history or, more recently,
"architecture." This is the new "social.")

So you can't just go out
and listen to the old tunes
blindly
         recording
eating things

         (I've always suspected the passive voice.
The object of the action has such a fiery breath. "Minimize
energy demand for heating and cooling – Go Passive."
Future simple and past continuous. Perfect the present is.)

Nobody lifts their eyes

Silence becomes the habit
Work will use up the cattle.
                              Their fields
phyla of proprioception.

                    (The pastry in the Sapir–Whorf
hypothesis is "technician." How you think is the writing on
the boards. Really, you could discover the truth. But the
noumenous is phenomenal. How the idea
          is to be perfect
                              the goal
          the body.)

123

The fulcrum of things
lengthened by narrative
thin line strung told
for example, season
and stone, twisted
words as roots, raked
"flax" the edge of prairie
and lake, shore lining
brim of dish spills the "I"
story's pushed surface
planar geography's lie
the way truth's worded
underneath horizon un-
parted sky unsung intent

124

All ways come back to sky
cows dream the marsh
back to Winnipeg, salt
city to Gimli seven cells
of history one at a time
another document lost
a third lights a track, takes
forth into the body blood
and then no more smoke
six others, like wolves
so we need torches, pitch
burning difference finally
oars as thick as two bys
drums about your head

125

Down past sliding home
north south to circle story
artery of the sentence saying
turn, turn around the sun
frozen above the intersection
at noon, inertia of a hawk
then behind and beyond mind
annexed in anecdote nowhere
but the middle of south
that highway to its sun
or some reef from lake
to feathers the line of poem
pecking at the edge of map
home honed its fuel glowed

126

And she would one day Dad had been told
I guess the biggest Loki said tore that birch
from an edge of ice scaled the pickerel badly
but it was too late I was on my way now the
rhythm apart from stars we were tired and
we met talking on the stoop those geese too
and their morning ruckus scoop to dream
I'm now an empty blue sky I took that picture
willows yellowed in the October morning
but I didn't go back there on the other side
of the field she said the net that cows become
frozen in the night sky the shape of raw spring
creeks knowing that this happens over and
objects can be anyplace like this ash beside me

127

The plateau of the poem
pulling a story from a fire
smouldering under foot
on a periphery of words
as things while sentenced
to a periphery of counting
so nearly uncontained (it)
documents no geography
nor memory the windmill
street and all that walks
or reminds crankshaft, smoke
sits at the corner cheering
past the end of telling you
can smell the stones burning

128

Dada Anna Blue

Oh lie me 27 in, Oh yes, do lie me
Do diner tick doe roll deer dust clear, – Hear!
Oh, do go lightly don't
mind me twenty
seven sins and
likely let's have more.

Do dine her
squeeze her count her
her and
her, but where?

Do best do worst
lie spoonin' here
but ride the blinds
and night with her.
Do diner trick doe roll deer dust clear, – Hear!
Lemon, yes, we're skin.

How are ya biscuit leaf
shakin' in the rust
jes' call red luck
You'll be another bloom.

Oh yes, oh yes, do lie me do.
Do diner tick doe roll deer dust clear, – Hear!
On the line.

Press fresh Anna
put another on her hat
blue's to die for groans
so vocal yes to kiss her.
anna – nanna – nAH!

Nana Anna whom?
Do diner tick doe roll deer dust clear, – Hear!
Dining on your name
before and after dinner.
You then You Yours truly I'm there.

Oh I know you know it Anna
honey dripper do salty rider
ANNA NANA BLUE
Do drop to here
I love your you yours!
Here and here and here.

128.1

from Schwitters's *Und* no political or social meaning
knot or note for Nietzsche's Gay Scientist
Dreaming from Magritte's *The Reckless Sleeper* 1927
some mind-work as a mirror
Egypt actually discovered that birdlike symmetry
(but for the "T" over her head)
and then pawprint loses out to glassiness (apples)
tree

129

citizen, vb. as in to citizen, -zening, -zened, -zens. To mix, to cross, to cast, to struggle, to represent, to justify, to place, to breathe, to own, to migrate, to alienate, to rescale, to trans-, translate, transcreate, transnationalize, to transgress, and so forth, to inflect, to inflict, to touch, to share, to experience, to tell the truth (the way the words lie), to domesticate, to inhabit, to escape, to dislocate, to image the nation, to imagine relation, to fragment, to serve the self, to fake, to gesture, to multiply, to name, to choose, to politicize, to cultivate, to read/write, to deterritorialize, to believe, to improvise, to consume, to torque, to screw, to unfix, to loosen, to listen, to practice, to see through, to appear or perform, to articulate, to equivocate, to shop, to co-opt, to know, to inform, to demand, to strip, to separate, to reclaim, to constitute, to hybridize or disappear

130

Roy Kiyooka Jumped Calgary

... "final surge of sap"
three months into Western Canada High School 15 years
old December 7, 1941 rebirth Japanese Pearl Harbor east
Calgary Switzer's corner Canadian store corner coke radio
sputtering how many Nisei nights cold pith of Opal's stars
and frozen fields

> "a small 'i' felt as if a punitive fist kept clenching
> and unclenching behind my back but each time I
> turned to catch it flexing it would disappear into the
> unlit corners of our small log house"

hapless breath
cross enemy alien
birthright erased

unimpeachable body

                    caws

> "I milked the cows churned the cream fed groomed
> and harnessed the horses rode the plough walked
> behind the disc and harrow cut each winter's supply
> of wood and hauled it home from the govt. wood
> lot. I helped birth pigs and calves and I helped the
> hired stallion hump our mares each spring"

voice on the phone
just passing through
otherwise
no trace
can't resist this westness

                   out there prairie "face
the same world
'Left' is
as 'Right' is"

           jump 1946 Cow Town
art high and given

                  out

                        West is
as East is *"hooping"* thimbleful

not "final surge"
            but gap

130.1

Glenbow's sensation of the body femin
<u>ism</u> made for thirst

some guy's art wire heart
post-marble still thinking nature/natural

uptitled I was made for having
lapped "at" her tears or wars

131

latches of summer

mind on to
Nippon
June 1986
Winnipeg acute
yet drifting

go no later
than Saturday
14th
qué es doble ve?
Thursday
meeting morning

protein hazards
all airborne
father's day
in Kochi
haze
from the mill
still visible

expo
for the apostroff
"¡"
minute
truthful
and particular

backyard

off Keefer
above MacLean
Park
just audible
drift
rock muzak
decayed
by decade

cbc under
yr skin
"my numen"
from Brilliant
to the bluffs
Cole or no
Porter

the king
a kind of
indenture
a replication
forged
and buried
"seemingly
implacable

surface" iteration
of black hair
hidden

lattices
of "we"
asian-canucks
spiffy
and industrial

pears ripen
above
the small
white pickup's
canopy
clouds moireéd
above
"our" mountains

impasto postcard
"his" "Tein-Choo"
"on the rack
at Octopus"
astonished
rib
just visible
replication

can't quite
retire
his pedagogy
nor zerox
the handsome
pension plan
yet Art's

"sheer brevity

of breath"
the Sproule Creek
of pituitary chakra
destroying rose
after rose
latticework
summer
after summer's
"supine tingle"

r-i-f-f riff
or as this
these "i's"
tilt (slant)
peacock-wise

not to copy
but to cry
this town out
traced
(he'd say)
"of an ancient
rectitude"

132

Curls

The girl on the left tells the girl on the right the story of her
life just like thick smoke curling up a chimney and is a little
surprised that it has up to now come to this sitting on a
beach or bent over in front of a campfire with only this twist
of a story or even their stories since the girl on the right finds
herself almost in the same story yet not wholly intersecting
with who they are and have always been except these girls
now have history and can remember the world in certain
shared ways they gossip about as in this *bavardage* that is
one of those moments in their stories or should we say since
they are looking right at one another tossing the stony and
smoky words back and forth that this right now is their story
(do they meander) and certainly as anyone who really reads
a photo can tell there are certain physical similarities these
two girls have probably always shared though they haven't
known one another for all their lives only since they became
young women howsomever as over-the-shoulder readers we
(including me) are pretty sure they will eventually become
older women because their curly hair can make us think
that rust should be white unless we get thrown for a loop
but anyway here they are at some point in their corkscrew
lives becoming older not old since that is a word that might
be hard to swallow later on in life though that is not even
part of the convoluted story at this moment in the smoke
of the campfire or her fingers entwined round the pebbles
falling into her hand or twisting the lid of the thermos to
pour another cup of tea that word they'll put aside to maybe

use toward the end of the story when the plot gets too complicated to remember but all we know by now is that they could get a kink in their necks wrapped up in the story of her life she keeps telling to the girl on the right she has discovered just won't stop and she can't figure it out it won't come together maybe she's been thrown a curve and it's not a story but a really beautiful poem coiling the syllables each new line touching the tongue as each word even the word old rolls off the tip right there in the moment of itself being the full spiral that hums into the *denouement* of their naturally curly lives

133

Someone to Be

If on time, my rocks
south of here transistor traced KNBC
Salt Lake City starry nights late
those heavenly maps, or wanting them
thought of here up against this shore
imagine who you could be then
or where
running ahead of yourself
triggered from the silver radio
read the score the day after
continuity favours the seasons
and festivals, even pachinko tries
to make of its stainless ball an icon
looking at her black hair from behind
in the parade of dying
isn't that the fashion? Summer
always draws to a close, but back
in the mouth the pungent ginger
roasting on the hibachi, wonder who
talks about that dream, someone
to be so much.

134

Looks like Summer

But too slow
those long late afternoon shadows
spacy, and alone, so alone
forgotten but not lost
they're out there hidden
daytime planets in the sun
fans hum at the back
of the dark matinee
ball glove folded into the plush
the cheerleaders' skirts in sync
will it be hit over the fence
but this is Kyoto
I've heard of it, pink hats
blond dye almost orange
that's just taste
     these disgraces are
      our graces
play ball at the Ginger Bowl
that alternate current
saving the words
for a winter's night

135

Inside the World

Inside the world
the ferry departs on time
mid-June until September.

Is it that you do
time in Pacific Time or
is the world a chamber of

border across the ocean
in those other languages
the schedule whittles to a fine point

phanopoeia. Clouds migrate
over the mountains, and then
the stars come out. Large

prepositions especially
our diaspora
measured as tree rings

harmony of the growing sky
at dusk. Then it's winter, alone
we all wait for the next one.

The promise of ocean: dry land.
I try to resist talking about
myself. But not to myself.

136

Dancing

Told me that feelings were like shoulders
used to say there was kindness in growing
but didn't ask to see the filling or the stuffing
so finally the apples fell off the tree
you see them and suddenly clap hands
this after having bitten but not eaten, then
Jack wrote the song "Shine on Harvest Moon"
the one where flesh is held close in dancing
a little different than testing the potatoes
when I asked him if he had booked a shot
he told me fish under the creek swam
the song debuted first as "Slung Tics of Policing"
downtown it was hand-to-mouth and hand-over-hand
all around the gym we counted without thinking
One two three Two two three
tried to keep our feet moving, it was
he said, the arithmetic of sadness

137

A Mineral Desire

He steeps raging though you sleep
deep or deeper, deeply than a clarinet
sudden white chest hairs, same old chin
should anyone else know, then let them
know the score, exactly, exacter
than the syllable in a poem feels faster
in the middle voice, you look back
and let the sleeping words lie
this isn't New Mexico, a mineral desire
deep in Sandia, hollow nibs of licorice
is how you earn your milk

138

Ex

Somewhere along the trail the eyes explode
on the lakeside where memory's anchored

bright orange tiger lily, like a saint
with bark. Exactly

clumps timed to perfection
the universe a lined history

that's a joke, reading the tea leaves
nothing British about it

not even the procedure or the machine
the way hiking is a matter of cartography

not memory, as represented by the fish
a subterranean word with a cedar accent

random depth charges of colour left over
chemistry when the work really begins

let's put a handle on the blood, ketchup
should not be pronounced with an accent

139

Bang

More than once it could be a tsunami
on another shore where old cousins used to live
chipping the social among the brightest stars
but thinking of it just like that, a year till the next
spark when the darkness would *really* unite, counting
the days left, counting the next move.

It was like a poke in the gut, this new story
padding the waves, the thinking, working it out
which meant deftly avoiding the tushes of intention
the kind of music that turns into an earworm
another Shinto idea entirely, washing, where
not who.

This other purpose faked its phosphorescence
it drifted across the ocean as a petri dish
or learned to pronounce the words for chemistry in Chinuk
Wawa.

140

Having tried trumpet stutter up front
as a slip of the tongue

as the length of meaning fades
adjust the lips

on every second note
you learn something

the fingering in the stomach
much like the taste of metal

these are the keys to this grave
C, G, A-flat
B, F, F-sharp
                    – major

each valve is designed to extend
the moment of language – as they say

if she plants in the spring
they eat in the fall.

140.1

Jennifer whoever
in the garden, nautical
post-reflection

underwater person
or her daughters
embryo of typograph/glyph

idea eyesight builds up
and with light
from the surface
                    material

(dirt)
substance projection mathematical almost carried

via optical mixture
(points) on white on white

but you do that in a garden
that's what you do
you plant

141

david is a man who carries a triangle and mistakenly prints
two to one which he then submits to bpNichol dot ca david
is very familiar with his name yet david's in the stagnate city
called home could he be the you in the alphabet who sighs
at the wrong love song who writes on the long road if david
is less you more me

142

Oh God please give us
a second chance
we'll hit the nail
square on the head
we'll dance for love
instead of shadows
if you'll forget
our other prayers
we'll build a house
out of bananas
something concrete
we can hang onto
turn the plans
into the body
tap the feet
into their soles.

We'll tear it down
and start again
do it right
make no mistakes
swing the hammer
kick the door
if we could have
another go

we'd never take no
and never say die
we'd teach our kids
to take a stance
live all the lines
build with stone
Oh Lord won't you give us
that second chance

i's pitch pipe the necessary deictic to the speaking event's absolute moment or epidemic index of the idea is to be perfect genitive also known as the infamous "Patient Zero" a designation whose tense has become a rolling St One just to remind us that "They're still here!!" this icon is as old as a racehorse just another temporal succession called "A Singer's Hell" but we hums same old same old in F minor just witness the "Stars and Stripes" identical to the founding colonies' arrows, errors, eros of St. Valentine flying this severed portion of contagious magic alive alive O every so often repeating the absolute pitch of the self meditating on its own second chanceness if only she would play the 2×4 and hammer as the fragment surfaces into the mouth trap to decide and tumble counter-clockwise between tumbling and directed swimming no geometric chance because the cell evokes memories how the hell could they get home to the tomb he says the one I found but she does too shocked to learn of the flag as an emotionally surcharged problem OK cuz here and now only lasts three seconds that's why this text has proper pauses to emphasize that the 3-second time window appears to be fully used up though he intuitively keeps trying the holy road not the now-mistaken inchoate road so they needs the *Indicator indicator* to cymbalize the way to the honey crotch of dying while the chorus marches to the drum of we's snare

144

this is the love poem:
that is the symptom:
this is the footprint:
that is the clue:
this is the sand:
that is the footprint:
this is the trail:
that is the song:
this is the headlight:
that is the diagnosis:
this is the scat:
that is the index:
this is the referral:
that is the snapped twig:

this is the drop of oil in the water that metaphorically
becomes the manual of *Reconnaissance and Scouting*

this is the single black hair fluttering in a small piece of film
displayed in the headlines still in love wanting to find
the right way home

145

that in this life alone becomes complete it all looks done and
zeroed in on one a stony stone a perfect single rock we be
sunk down becoming moan

that in this life the stranger seems to be the only one in town
who knows the song the one that starts with "Oh" and ends
"Just passing through"

that in this life the pronoun's heart breaks i to you and triple
tongues a "me me me" whose echoes overlap inflected
waves of them, us, they, and we

that in this life when the meaning's over and the dog heads
down to the creek when the ol' man's gone and the lights go
out the last leg falls asleep when one turns to zero thinking's
complete just before the end of its sentence

146

Slant likely the essential archive alley Alberta at least Piikani
(not the brick factory quiet on a Saturday afternoon) but
between wood + brick walk sudden shade no sooner so
necessary to the story but it's bedtime among the acacia +
some crickets remember the novel is dynamite, that "tough
trip through paradise," Beckett thought such blending aside
not to mention on seeing at that very moment the participial
connection Flouncing

147

Slant into an impossible French Me those luminous venetians
their light propelled by the heat shimmering from the red
brick above the dry cleaners at that very moment the
afternoon *toujours* with cousins an absolute translation
of ancestry not + beyond which an occasional "Darling"
assembles itself on the wire aware of a secret syntax buried
in a knot of class + spoken subjects not to mention *la suie* +
the scant wipe as the slat bends + you can see the smelter
on the hill across the river

148

Slant apostrophe of absent minded thinkin' even 'memberin'
th' lyrics to "Look for the Silver Linin'" was it not Chet who
dialed that Jezebel while I spent th' weekend in Fernie
lookin' for Melody her peakin' through th' striated venetians
at th' Royal thinkin' 'bout her 'quipment humpin' my elbow
oh + then shared her Cameo draggin' thru a kiss all th'
way back to town flyin' low still as we walked into th' café
laughin' 'n jivin' high 'bout Saturday night

149

Slant instrument of heaven. Up there cloud swings
between. Some hoodlums holding. A dozen white blouses.
Permeating a few of its threads. Gladly, either memory sees
nothing: the mother + the father. Faking less stairway. Under
door. The eyes right there, thereing. Akokli [goat] Creek.
Melody lingers. – *He'll be back at the end of the summer,
won't he?* Hand over fist. Never a duck's fart. Them. Like the
rest + that wild blue yonder with no particular spot to hit

150

Slant Obit singing sentence pov junctions intone primary
stress incl. all space + things th' body intersects where
appearance knows house cracking ground morph of syntax
same prime *noumen-* passing through just like Hermes did
tuwhit silence sounds so blue no matter she says every
word same meaning but also accelerator into th' full-as-
it-gets story even memory blows th' chords away into th'
then what happened next since all appliances humming so
ya can freeze cook 'n see all self appearance recognition
unimportant to th' prime turns in narrative how flying all
over th' sky of open-mindedness th' *who* poking *what*
then holding tight to th' word in mind like breathing out +
breathing in still I wondering 'bout th' *eme* as th' indigene of
paradigmatic thought suffixing just that apropos of leaving
no trace like those chords that appear by disappearing into
some kind of permanent rhyme *vis* family concoction *avec*
sleeping insects in veins passing major/minor frets fingers
only momentarily hesitate before they grab a share of th'
fold past old chilling patience of th' fiction vendors stalled
out by too lean a mix in Choate Road we all trying to plug
into inchoate wrld a *uta* without a *nikki* beyond that th'
chase goes on into "Polka Dots and Moonbeams" "speaking
of heartless purveyors" of th' dashboard some phantom
wahhhh from beyond th' firewall echoes a jargon of late-
night loneliness remembering thinking is th' music you'll
always sing to th' ~~concocted~~ trajectory of mistranslation
floating + drifting through th' desire to begin again

150.1

"Bagatelle for Albers"
"Pennies from Heaven"!

no not colour
leading out along the road late
to catch the last ferry
maybe the eyes (smoke) hint

(pink
and the shapes slippers
Jed August
moon
Kate

151

Medallions of Belief

stranger music copyrights end of
the band that wanders through the car's FM
under an on-the-move cloudy foothills sky
ostranenie
                    the future torture servants have the code
the black man's gone – there'll be *no* more dirty dancing
Sunday school wasn't enough, that Italian suit you wear
has pockets full of snuff
                    all those "if you don'ts" they warned
might still be sudden summer storms
and if you are that stony stone
that thinks it gets to watch the show alone
then go to Granny's house and dial
a distant prairie station.

emblematic parachutes of a world
free-floating in that old eternal breeze
the compact disc of Western Civ
and meaning
                    somewhere
in the American southwest
between Santa Fe and Placitas, say,
maybe somewhere outside of Tucson,
the enemy-friend holes up.

But we never get the song about the Toyota Land Cruiser.

Instead, the train and Lili Marlene plot the transit gaze
and axis through Berlin
no bumper shoot required.

We only seek to adjust our birthmarks
to the modulations of poetic order
and disaster.

? (period)
of revenge for skin and signal haze.

"Bring Back the Birch" Little Sparta
sing that anthem: "Could my 'ing' be my 'ang'?"

New government, new syntax.
Brawl, not.

The tactic of parenthesis
fence and gate.

151.1

February sun hot car melting radio from see bee sea ekphrastic stilling in the damp headliner air with the windows rolled down to parity as a go-between Hank Bull's AM art echoes Bob and Ray wishing "you folks in radioland could see these photographs" phantopoeic ventriloquist hum through the poplar branches snow giving way to Gombrich's apatropaic image just some wood chipped away, feet to a table, claws, just above the dashboard, waves

152

Turn Left Wing Albuquerque

You are the key, the prize too
Too many letters for Scrabble
But your eyes are tired from staring away from the sea
You can't see the trees for the desert
Think about it, death's not a question
Trade Empire for another wing
You're so powerful, you do not want the under
That would be meaning
Turn down that road and don't step on the grass
And don't fly away angry

152.1

At Sea
so green the red, John, border
w/ words, "the" words
                   AT SEA
water a green somewhere
suggests blues
as in crayons, World
Wieners by Ron Kitaj
Leatherstocking on the wall of the Kyoto British Council
"Lapis Lazuli," light food up the dark alleyway
1966, 1938. Steaming. Steering.

153

Person 1

quest or guest
shadow or meadow
emblem or blaming
fog for an hour
myth or message
sphingical or chilling effects
her stare hysterical
remembering the future
heteronym or a British Columbian
fatal or fade out
agonize or Greek eyes
persuade or pout
crest or wave
shield or shyed
pretending or defending
motto or lotto
ocean to ocean

154

Accident

    Come both
        apple mouth
    Act from double destination
    Defend your memory of the tongue
    Then argue w/ the facts
        of outraged Africa.

    Your mouth did tear the skin
    Accidental bear in tree
    For all the science and
        the body of outside
    The apple mouth that opens
        w/ a word that bites.

    This isn't the truth
    Breaks the branches
    Plato's cave is dark too
    (yet has a hand in every mouth)
    It is that mouth that chews the conduct
        of your eye.

155

Person Dom

Midnight, can't sleep, so writing you this letter.
In which I plant my love
Familiar murmur, but you can't hear the silence.
The words rumour the harvest of pines
Nation locked out by the beetle.

The song of our lake is so pure
        we can drink it.
Ocean of us.

Talk of forest and tides, distances.
"older but knowing no better
still in love, wanting
that good song to be sung
inging it ahead into the dark
beyond the high beam
hoping"

156

Ode to Castles Out

The face that stares,
a coat spelled out.

The oriental accident just fits a better country
Rampant told the Lion and the Unicorn
To go out on a limb and hold

A coat of arms out at the elbows
A river out of wandering
At first it is a useful coat
out of sun, snow, rain, and prairie wind
As tidy as England's ponds and fashion
Among us roasting maple leaves and thistles

It fits, coming from the sulphur of Saskatchewan
Out west, step off the edge

This rope is just the ribbon of desire

157

A Vanished Nocturne

Such a headache
ghost pilings no longer
log booms in sight

that beautiful white dog
of the night
just a casino of stars

how to arrive
deep into this remark
old sketch erased
between Sundays
mostly rain

but this is the skin
of an old Europe
soft ashes
of the afternoon singing
from C to C

158

Epitaph

Here is the lie:
        the shore is always small and changing
The Captain of Contain. Drunk, in awe.
Don't be afraid; we're mesmerized to analogy.
The last one picked is highest in the tree.

159

Top notch how could *Mountain* be steel town drive into
adolescent transnational mimeo mind reached out through
this polluted shore of the great lake who could tell such
a personal story through the poem one needs daughters
even when you lead a gypsy life kicking east west until the
wee vision of Scots Canadian intention turned up as side-
street hospitality that day our VW bus broke down and she
needed feeding where was the anyone of the mind then
until you left town again in that high-hope sonnet you could
chew on

159.1

On this side is space

This side is blank

On this side is freedom

This side is blank

On this side is emptiness

This side is on the other side

On this side is arriving

This side is lava

On this side is an ocean

Which side do we drive on

Over here is doubt

This side is an afternoon

On this side there are ankles

We think we see cows

On this side is the sky

On this side is ice cream

On this side are the trucks

Over there's a different pronoun

This side is for lost and found

On this side we sigh

This side is for walking

Just as windy on this side

This side can be cold

This side is dreaming

This side is for windows

On this side is the future

This side is almost full

On this side the door is open

This side is thinking ahead

This side is windy

On this side are lies

As far as you can see

On this side is thinking

This side is here

Between us is the river

This side remembers the future

On this side is a creek

This side is possible

This side is in your face

This side is migration

On this side are scarves

But they're just rocks

On this side is a stroller

Keep to the right

On this side are the bicycles

This side is waiting

On this side we talk

This side is for maps

Over here we say hello

This side is for crying

On this side is repeating

This side can be strict

Up ahead are the horses

On this side is the number

This side can't help it

I am standing in the doorway

Live is what we will do later while we wait for the riffs to
become rifts and shock us to attention tongue sudden soon
as the chord of silence takes over is this "Perdido" the words
just stop and your eyes glaze wait for the next beat and it
could end there but then a *then* rolls such sweet thunder up
into an arpeggio we've never heard before out of time only
a syllabic river of sound breaking up into speech clouds the
dissonant air hypnotic you've talked non-stop through your
vision but now you've paused on the bridge listening, not
lost at all but listening

161

Not another's trap but just our own magic mountain map
doesn't replication help the mind as if it were a selfie of
regret remorse gratitude shame to do it blind like Twombly
drawing in the dark intention fell back into the aperture
where the lines became worn paths you know the kind
that beckon and I could see myself but not the honesty of
gesture hopefully that'll come later and I'll remember I'm not
alone and even if it's just a game trail I can trust the animal
eyes that see it in the dark

161.1

emergency of maps
shape of puddles
fruit of wards
pith of whales

162

Notate the body to make a phrase of shape
but of varied possibilities thought
swoop ...
...
clouded and lost in the striate of white grey nacre wanting
so much to blow the truth of the body
into this moment through this stem

163

A bird in the hand etcetera the berries of deixis reply here
and here between thumb and index rolls over waiting
mouths happy choice for the stem of abundance hold this
moment of transit in choice another and another there and
there at eleven hundred and twenty metres a cup of sound
that is memory yes that one the song in the trees behind me

164

a stony stone or just some other stone   to
point me at itself
    iting itself at the fire there
burns   and looks

165

Now is an elusive thing i
                              ignored
and not what it does to thought nor used
as a measure   re posed as memory   knock
at the door
                        out there   come in
report for duty

166

Ever notice how a bird points to itself
                    is that a kind of itself question
            a colour or a song a branch
now listen with the sky   didn't I tell you

167

this river shifts shaking raven who novels under them those
stories   just as soon walk
the mind   back there as fall into
                    a reservoir
empty lake between two rivers

168

I point to my own absolute experience of
myself as a step towards which all
my being flows (into) & fills
and from that there a physical place
out of which the possible ...

... just so there's a steady flow of breath
of him who is the turbine of his own sources
and comes from the base of the neck
from a small hint of light
far back of what is about to happen

(marking the spot as a ritual
sitting on a log waiting to get lost
that was the time the mind walked
between where they were
and what will not bend
when telling the truth so cold
she said I can't whistle
to keep the bears away
her sentence won't be the dash
to connect then to soon
stop look and listen here
yes here between the words)

169

Before Loki was buried at Smoky Creek he pointed at the
water because it is a magnet that suddenly hurries to rescue
his stomach shook his fur was cold then ran through the trees
and field under the large sky of night followed him to the
creek smelled immediate that whole moment was for joining
his own body fell into breath into mouth in this way it was
toward *The* song waited for

170

Presence

About that smoke around your neck about the invitation
you expect to be delivered to your door the one that creaks
but can't be locked then opens where the rabbit plague
began and mythology inherited another story of discovery
with a monkey in it leaping all over the violence in the gems
of boundary where we had been trying to live a year or
two and then set sail for El Dorado westward even though
the smoke was heavy in Oregon and British Columbia
obliged then to wait until mid-afternoon in the old Atlantic
time somewhere in the Pacific this was also the rule in that
hemisphere where the discipline of the anecdote waited
for the ending in the music or the hum of electric light rigidly
enforced in the silent middle voice because the law of halves
looks on both sides of the imaginary circle around the earth
which never stops polishing and sweetening the celestial
sphere no crack no opening of any sort but very bright where
medicines no longer have any helpful effect so there it was
in the pattern of the cigar metaphor storyfied just like from
the days of the Canadian remittance man just like the circle
waits for the cheque at the month's end just as the tidy brain
gets shipped or shopped around the world at least the one
we read about and take for proof there's no escape from
this equator of thought and appearance for example at
noon there's lunch at the Great meridian and there is waiting
waiting for the chalk line of recognition even though I have
to approach it at a long slant I would rather see it than any
other thing in the world girdle the doldrums even bring it

back to Lew Welch's *Wobbly Rock* and that charcoal border
we talked about are these the stamps for the final envelope
a condition of things findable elsewhere in the tricky slant
of echo repeating as an augmented fourth forwards and
backwards plus minus stretched out across the ocean which
the sailor described to the young girl as a sluggish 20 degree
blue ribbon through which the ship slows down as it climbs
up the bulge at the centre of the planet even told her that one
must shave when crossing the equator for the first time but he
didn't tell her about Neptune's intervention into our own solar
system of facts e.g., this morning we are in the night of time
which will last far longer than day and tomorrow we'll be
close to the centre of our imagination and then have to drop
out a day never knowing how much time remains until we get
to fade out in the coda forget about the equinox thoughts of
this kind are always tomorrow along about the moment we
cross over the meridian or at least invent that movement in
order to find the honesty of history who can remember the
citizen of our own Big sky Dipper used to be called Great
Bear until it became the property of the United States trying
to MAGA the universe but no more talk of riots having
crossed the celestial boundary now the Southern Cross will
need a sky all to itself so sayeth Sam Clemens:

I would not change the Southern Cross to the
Southern Coffin, I would change it to the Southern
Kite; for up there in the general emptiness is the
proper home of a kite, but not for coffins and
crosses and dippers.

Beneath the Magellanic Clouds lies the bell bird of

recognition ringing out at short intervals from behind
the constant whooshing of a deep wind avoiding the
miscalculation of overdensity where should we be for solace
within this perfect fiction the withering heat from the NE
brings on stupendous drought tracking its own thread of
dementia through the doldrums under a constant ringing of
each note in the augmented interval of Krakatoa's equatorial
smoke stream or westward river of Indonesian exhaust or
Quito's breathless haze chased into the hillsides smoldering
in Sumatra now that the Amazon's part of the desire for
new news burning at the hemline where presence is where
it should be right in the middle if the map has no beginning
just the skirt of our globe dressed up for the plan of our
violence if the plan is the body moved by those clouds of
Brazilian smoke then each of the *presidentes* drift to the
equator's inner chamber where doubloons cast in silicon
dress their greedy skin each cold layer embossed with
magnetic poetry under a *Star Wars* letterhead and the
incessant sonic booms of natural resources pave the way
for the next cricket farm while the bells keep ringing and
the confessional curtain rustles not revealing its dark secrets
but our knees are getting sore our penitence don't help
while standing in the doorway you could oil the creaking
hinges with dinosaur memory or that little yellow sticky
on the fridge door reminding us of the same song every
day deep time looms out there are wrinkles in that thread
through the middle kingdom of celestial garbage and a
showy imperfection in the asphalt of the imagination always
trying to economize the truth as another *Treasure Island* let's
confess and live under the bridge since distance is presence
dammit where is my copy of *America: A Prophecy* is this the

chain of memory that resurrects Albion's cliffs is this where I'm supposed to meet you is this the door that's never locked is this the creek where Loki died is this river just the smoke around my neck and if so why not make the smoke a door

Note

The first edition of *Music at the Heart of Thinking*, 1–69, was published by Red Deer College Press in 1987.* The project was provoked by a request from bpNichol, in the early '80s, for material for an *Open Letter* series that he and Frank Davey were editing, on "notation."† I sent them eleven "MHTs," including an introductory note that explains:

> In the explication of these estranged pieces lies possible coherences for some sense of writing as a notation for thinking as feeling. The difficulty is literal and intentional. I'm wary of any attempt to make it easy – "language (the true practice of thought)," Kristeva says ...‡

The "MHTs" became, for me, a niche for a compositional attention I wanted to explore in particular ways. I had been attracted to the prose poem through my attempts at the *utanikki*, the poetic journal. Within the prose poem I was interested in upsetting the tyranny of the sentence as a unit of composition. The resistance to closure and syntactic predictability implicit in contesting the sentence is a dynamic also shared with the long poem.

---

*   *Music at the Heart of Thinking* (Red Deer, AB: Red Deer College Press, 1987).

†   *Open Letter* 5.2 (Spring 1982), 5.3 (Summer 1982), 5.7 (Spring 1984), 6.1 (Spring 1985), and 6.7 (Spring 1987).

‡   *Open Letter* 5.7 (Spring 1984), 33. The Julia Kristeva quote is from her essay "Word, Dialogue and Novel," collected in *The Kristeva Reader*, edited by Toril Moi (Hoboken, NJ: Basil Blackwell, 1986), 36.

The first sixty-nine were prefaced with this remark:

> The notion underlying *Music at the Heart of Thinking* comes from a Chinese movie I saw in Japan several years ago. It was a martial arts film about the Shao Lin monks in China. One of the monks would practice his tai chi while drunk so he could learn how to be imbalanced in the execution of his moves without falling over. In real battle his opponents were confused by his unpredictability. I've tried to use the same method in these pieces, *sans* booze of course. This method of composition is the practice of negative capability and estrangement I've recognized for many years through playing jazz trumpet, looking at art, and writing poetry. I've tried to use it here in a series of improvisations on translations of and critical writing about contemporary texts and ideas.

Apropos of "improvisation," this exchange from an interview[*] by rob mclennan explains the origin of that compositional impetus for me:

> **Q:** What is it about William Carlos Williams's *Kora in Hell: Improvisations* (1920) that has been so important to your work? Is it purely the fact of introducing you to the possibilities of improvisation, or does it go beyond that?

[*]   rob mclennan, "A Short Interview with Fred Wah," *Jacket 2*, March 5, 2015, jacket2.org/commentary/short-interview-fred-wah.

A: I was introduced to the possibilities of improvisation through the immediacy of composing a "moment" while *ad libbing* on the trumpet in a high-school jazz band. Williams came a little later, around 1961, as an affirmation of an improvisational condition, or possibility, in writing. I picked up a copy of Number Seven of the City Lights Pocket Poet Series *Kora in Hell: Improvisations* at Duthies downtown for a buck and a quarter. I had been turned on to Williams's "The Desert Music," which we had looked at in Warren Tallman's 406 Poetry class at UBC.

At the time, I didn't contextualize *Kora* historically (first published in 1920; I didn't see *Spring and All*, 1923, until later). What I read was syntactic noise. The text rambled wonderfully all over the place, the writing and the writer in sync with each linguistic moment, totally open and unpredictable: "When beldams dig clams their fat hams (it's always beldams) balanced near Tellus' hide ..." etc., not narrative but focused on the word, the syllable, the sounds, the phrase (rubbing against the sentence). I didn't register "prose poem" formally until later, with *Music at the Heart of Thinking*. But that drive in the syntax, non-sequential, non-sensical, the edges of phrase and word, provided me with a clear sense of the units of composition I was interested in playing and exploring.

As Roy Miki describes, "Unpremeditated and unplanned as it

was, *Kora* ... showed Williams that a writer composes *as he writes*."[*] Ever since reading, in 1960, Charles Olson's admonition that "in any given poem always, always one perception must must must MOVE, INSTANTER, ON ANOTHER!,"[†] I've been interested in engaging with the "kinetics" of the poem.

1–10 were written for and published in an issue of *Open Letter* (5.7 [Spring 1984]) on notation. **MHT 21–30** were written for and published in a Festschrift for bpNichol (*Open Letter*, 6.5–6.6 [Summer–Fall 1986]). **MHT 40–49** were written for a special edition of a collection of writings for Warren Tallman (collected and published by Peter Quartermain, Fall 1986). **MHT 50–59** are series of meditations on bpNichol's *Martyrology* books five and six. Other pieces in **MHT 1-69** are responses to texts by Steve Rodefer, Gerry Hill, Michel Gay, George Bowering, Robert Kroetsch, Lionel Kearns, Nicole Brossard, Frank Davey, Dave McFadden, Steve McCaffery, Roy Kiyooka, and Phyllis Webb.

MHT 70–105 were collected by Red Deer College Press as *Alley Alley Home Free*[‡] and included the series "Artknots 1–33" (folded in and decimalized in this edition). Some of the texts are responses to Robert Kroetsch's "Delphi: Commentary" (1983), Salman Rushdie's *The Satanic Verses* (1988), Roy Kiyooka's *Pear Tree Pomes* (1987), Aritha van Herk's crypto-fictive

---

[*] Roy Miki, "A Preface to William Carlos Williams: The Prepoetics of *Kora in Hell: Improvisations*," abstract (Ph.D. diss., University of British Columbia, 1980).

[†] "Projective Verse," in *The New American Poetry*, edited by Donald M. Allen (New York: Grove Press, 1960), 358.

[‡] *Alley Alley Home Free* (Red Deer, AB: Red Deer College Press, 1992).

doppelgänger Hannike Buch,[*] and works by Charles Bernstein, Nicole Brossard, Jack Clark, Barry McKinnon, Duncan McNaughton, Karl Siegler, Christine Stewart, and Bill Sylvester.

MHT 106–170, written since the early '90s, seem more dispersed. Though they continue to be responses to texts, many of them are occasioned by a sense of seriality. Collecting them now for this edition, the aftertaste of the serial can be located in the kind of randomness that is important to writing as thinking that I found in Robin Blaser's *Syntax* (1983) and *Pell Mell* (1988).

119 "cat's cradle" is lifted from *Articulations*,[†] a collaboration with visual artist Bev Tosh. I've recycled it here to underline the materiality of improvisation: "I want to be free to use the crumbs and scraps for the crumbness and scrapness in them, for nothing else."

121 "Strangles" were written as "chimes" for my collection of essays *Faking It: Poetics and Hybridity*, edited by Smaro Kamboureli (2000). They reiterate a range of my poetic shrapnel transitioning into the expository.

140–145 are in response to *Ad Sanctos*, a choral performance work, bpNichol/words, Howard Gerhard/music, *The Martyrology Book 9, 1986–1987* (1993). "Book 9" is the last published segment of bpNichol's lifelong poem. In the summer of 1988, just before his untimely death, I discussed with him loose plans he had for further books of *The Mart*, at that point projected into Book 13.

---

[*]   Published as *Snap* (Vancouver, B.C.: pomeflit, 1992).

[†]   Vancouver, B.C.: Nomados, 2007.

146–150: As I looked for a way to read into Gail Scott's novel *The Obituary* (2010), I realized the forms of composition and reception that opened for me resonated with the reading-writing dynamics I continue to consider in *Music at the Heart of Thinking.* This is not simply to contest the syntactic and the narrative, the two tyrannies of literature, but to be present to the galactic coherences that occur when we allow language to stumble over itself and we recognize that the synapses and disjunctions at the intersection of mind and word and perception shift, slant.

152–158 are transcreations of a Fernando Pessoa text I came upon in a bookstore in Lisbon. I used them in the context of a paper ("From C̀ to C: A Prepositional Poetics"*) I presented at "From Sea to Sea," a conference on Canadian literature. The Pessoa text is *Mensagem/Message,* translated by Jonathan Griffin, introduction by Helder Macedo (1992).

162–169 are conversations with Christine Stewart's *Treaty 6 Deixis* (2018), a series I could subtitle as "Exercises in Pointing." As Christine's text suggests, when we use words to point we must also listen. Her brilliant short essay "Treaty Six from under Mill Creek Bridge"† is pertinent to a poetics that seeks to reterritorialize the echoes of inherited forms and language.

170 is written for a collaboration with sound artist Magali Babin for *Chorus,* a poetic installation. It uses some material from the following sources: Mark Twain, *Following the Equator:*

---

* In *Ilha do Desterro* 56 (January–June 2009), 51–72.

† In *Toward.Some.Air.: Remarks on Poetics,* edited by Fred Wah and Amy De'Ath (Banff, AB: Banff Centre Press, 2015), 132–141.

A *Journey Around the World* (1897); Charles Olson's poem "The chain of memory is resurrection ..."; and Kaie Kellough, *Magnetic Equator* (2019).

Some of the other pieces sidle up to Roy Kiyooka, Leonard Cohen, Kurt Schwitters, Daphne Marlatt, George Bowering, David Arnason, David McFadden, Doug Barbour, and Sharon Thesen.

I know this is not an easy poetry to read; it wasn't easy to write. You're not intended to "get it." My hope is that you can share with me those detonations and silences we often unexpectedly come upon between words, syllables, letters, sounds, and rhythms: the minding and the music; the amulets of surprise coherence; the shapeliness of our imaginations at the threshold of language. Beware of that readerly inclination of "Voicing the sense, we fight against the tune ..."*

Acknowledgments

Some of the poems in this book have been published
by the following journals, anthologies, books, and small
presses: *Absinthe, Barscheit, Border Crossings, Boulder
Pavement, Brick, The Bulletin, Camrose Review, Canadian
Literature / Littérature canadienne, The Capilano Review,
Cross-Canada Writers' Quarterly, Dark Matter & Other
Radicals, The East Village Poetry Web, The Edmonton Bullet,
The False Laws of Narrative, filling Station, intent, Interlope,
Line, Massachusetts Review, Matrix, Measurements: Out from
Buffalo, Medallions of Belief; Michigan Quarterly Review,
Open Letter, Ós – The Journal, Philly Talks, Poesia do Mundo,
Poetry Australia, Poetry Canada Review and Chronicle,
Politics/Letters, PomFlits, Prairie Fire, Premonitions, Prism
International, Sagetrieb, Salt, Screens and Tasted Parallels,
Secrets from the Orange Couch, Slug Press, Somewhere
Across the Border, Temblor, Toward. Some. Air., TransLit,
Tripwire, Tyuonyi, West Coast Line, The White Wall, Words
We Call Home, Xconnect, Xcp: Cross Cultural Poetics,* and
Zest. Thanks to their editors. Thanks also to Nicole Brossard
for her kind permission to reprint her "Si Sismal."

I'm much indebted to Catriona Strang for her editorial
intelligence and guidance. Her understanding of and
familiarity with the book's compositional aspirations have
been generative and sustaining. Jeff Derksen's critical
attention to this work over many years has also reinforced
its orchestration, particularly his suggestion of an index
as an aid to reading. I hope, after publishing the first two
editions for Red Deer College Press when he was alive, that

Dennis Johnston might still enjoy the harmony. Reprinting those first two was Karl Siegler's idea and, happily, Kevin Williams has eagerly pursued the project. This is the third of my books designed by Leslie Smith and, once again, the book as an artifact strikes a unique chord. To Vicki, Spencer, Charles, Chloë, andrea, Rya, and Mocha, the whole Talonbooks choir, thanks for backing up poetry: music at the heart of thinking.

Index

1

1920 182
1922 76
1927 192
1938 228
1941 194
1944 33
1946 195
1949 6
1950 76
1954 9
1959 28
1961 58
1962 74
1966 228
1971 171
1977 171
1986 197
1987 171

A

abacus 119
Abbotsford 79, 81
Aeolus 92
A-flat 210
Agamben, Giorgio 174
A., John 44, 180
Akokli Creek 221
Albers, Josef 223
Alberta 150, 218
Albion 167, 251
Albuquerque 227
alterity 178–179
Amaryllis 100
America 52, 137, 148, 250
America, a Prophecy, William
    Blake 250
among 209, 218, 232
anima 35, 119, 147
animal 238
anthropology 35
apatropaic 226
apostroff 197
apple 35, 42, 44, 127,
    135, 230
aptic 5
arpeggio 237
asian-canucks 199

Athena 94
Atlantic 88, 110, 248
autumn 97

B

Baker, Chet 220
Bakhtin, M.M. 32
Banff 9, 140
Barthes, Roland 243
baseball 5
bavardage 111, 201
bear 35, 49, 61, 230, 249
Beckett, Samuel 218
Beckmann, Max 182
Berlin 225
Bernalillo 131
Beuys, Joseph 120
bicameral 17
biotext 121, 179
birch 188, 225
bird's nest soup 133
birth-breath 135
Blake, William 53–55, 92
Blow, Joe 65
Bolinas 62
border 79, 152, 156, 205,
    228, 249
boulder 40
Bowering, George 42, 121
brain 84, 86, 161, 248
breathing 17, 31, 135, 172,
    178, 222
bridge 34, 103, 125, 139, 145,
    170, 180, 237, 250
Brilliant 198
broccoli 106
Brossard, Nicole 157
Buch, Hannike 144
Bull, Hank 226
Burrard Street 170
Butterick, George 176

C

Cabot, Sebastian 49
cadence 128, 140, 179
café 96, 131, 220
Calgary 194
Cambodia 91, 180
Canada 68, 91, 142, 194

Canaan 91
candida 19
capability 13, 99, 116
car 9, 26, 57, 62, 64, 77, 94,
    108, 114, 224, 226
Carr, Emily 168
cartography 208
Castlegar 71
Castles 232
Cavalcanti 37
Caw 18, 133
CBC 137, 198
cedar-head 178
cellular 67, 112, 146
Cézanne, Paul 53
chain 72, 251
chakra 124, 200
chalk 6, 111, 174, 248
Champlain, Samuel de 49
Chilliwack 79
Chinaman 14
Chinatown 106, 133, 143
chink 168
Chinuk Wawa 209
Choate Road 222
ciliolum 175
circuit 3, 88
citizen 193, 249
Clarke, Jack 88
class 183, 219
clear-cut 154
Clematis Creek 176
code 113, 152, 155, 224
Coleman, Victor 81
Connecticut 177
containerism 117
Conversazione 58
Corman, Cid 79
cottonwood 42, 163
couloir 34, 75
cousins 179, 209, 219
Cow Town 195
coyote 70, 91
cradleness 173
Creekscape 72
Creeleyeye 64
Creeley, Robert 53, 60, 131

crow 69, 161
Cultus Lake 81
culvert 158

D

dadoed 61
Dal Lake 81
dance 13, 113, 120, 144, 213
daughters 70, 92, 101, 180, 211, 235
death 29, 31, 89, 107–108, 130, 227
defamiliar 13
deixis 241
de le Cosa, Juan 32
Delphi 90–91, 96
dementia 250
dendrita 144
deterritorialize 193
detour 79
diaphragmed 176
diaspora 205
difference 1–2, 38, 173, 186
dis-orientation 112
ditch 79, 97
Donne, John 64
door 100–102, 144, 151–152, 176, 180, 213, 221, 236, 243, 248, 250–251
Dorado, El 248
Dorn, Ed 68
downstream 97
driftwood 150
dromenon 13, 114, 117
drum 4, 68, 118, 146, 149, 176, 215
drunk 13, 79, 234
Duchamp, Marcel 9
Duncan, Robert 64, 103, 106

E

echo 71, 100, 126, 249
edge 13, 36, 86, 100, 105, 107, 112, 130, 137, 145, 169–170, 176, 185, 187–188, 232
egg 10, 81, 160, 178
Egypt 111–112, 192
elenxis 117
-eme-clutter 166
Empire 227

endomorphic 25
Enki 132
en route 26
entelecheic 127
Enyalion 122
Erika 137
Ernst, Max 14
eye-chaktra 132
eyes 8, 13–14, 23, 25, 30–33, 44, 77, 81, 83–84, 103, 132, 134, 149, 161, 163, 183, 208, 221, 223, 227, 229, 237–238

F

fake 13, 173, 193
family 114, 173, 183, 222
feather 18, 139, 179
Fenellosa, Ernest 65
Fernie 220
field 16, 20, 56, 74, 155, 188, 247
fir 18, 167
Fishstar 141
flap-and-squawk 116
Flouncing 218
foothills 224
foreignicity 128, 179–180
Fort Langley 79
fragment 16, 130, 152, 180, 193, 215
Frank Slide 165, 176
Fraser Valley 79
Fred 72
Freddy 159
French 7, 16, 19, 37, 51, 142, 219
From Feathers to Iron, John Clarke 103
F-sharp 210
f-stop 93

G

gabble 100
Gaian 125
genetic 35, 77, 103, 123, 125, 178
geomance 72
Gerber, Joanne 19
German 50
Ghat 81
Gimli 186

ginger 117, 122, 180, 203–204
glacier 20, 47
glyph 72, 211
Gombrich, Ernst 226
grammar 15, 77, 100, 112, 141, 149
Granny 77, 224
gravel 10, 46, 104, 116, 127, 135, 158
Green Door 151
gyna 122

H

hackled 145
half 8, 43, 66, 141
half-bred 159
Harebell 176
Harrison, Jane Ellen 13
Hastings Street 180
hawk 30, 40, 187
heart-clock 176
Helen 8
Heraclitus 175
Hermes 86, 91, 96, 134, 151, 222
Hesiod 90
heterocellular 102
Hill, Gerry 20
Hindmarch, Glady [Maria Gladys] 79
history 14, 38, 43–44, 51–52, 78, 110, 112, 121, 140, 162, 164, 173–174, 183, 186, 201, 208, 249
hologrammar 10
home 57, 75, 79, 94, 102, 119, 133, 135, 148, 150, 172, 178, 180, 187, 194, 212, 215–216, 249
homome 111
horologicals 67
horse 3, 15, 42, 81
huckleberry 172
hunger 16, 35, 60, 82, 114, 118, 123, 148
hunt 4
hybridize 193
hyphen 100, 109, 179

I

icefield 162

Ikebukuro 76
inchoate 34, 75, 215, 222
Indiana, Robert 58
indigene 222
inging 5, 231
interior 37, 82
interpellation 175
Irene 51
isness 98
istory 145–146

J

Japan 62, 68, 79, 90
jazz 106, 138, 151
Jennifer 211
journeying 37, 40

K

Kachina 162
Kamboureli, Smaro 178
Kansas 161
kapow 118
Keefer Street 198
Kerényi, Károly 93
Kerouac, Jack 64
kerykeion 95
kick-the-can 119
kinaesthesis 118
Kitaj, Ron 74, 228
Kiyooka, Roy 42, 72, 90,
    132, 170, 194
KNBC 203
knot 14, 93, 103, 125, 146,
    174, 180, 192, 219
knowing 3, 22, 25, 99–100,
    116, 124, 156, 178, 188,
    231, 249
Kochi 197
Kootenay 71, 78
Kora 87
krino-sift 148
Kristeva, Julia 37
Kroetsch, Robert 64, 77
kulchur 180
Kwakwaka'wakw 31
Kyoto 23, 204, 228

L

labyrinth 1, 92, 101, 103,
    180
Lac des Entouhonorons 73
lacrosse 20
lake-nests 21

language 1, 7, 16, 19, 27, 37,
    48, 67, 78, 87, 89–90, 98,
    123, 133, 136, 147, 156,
    210
lapis 176, 228
laughin' 220
Leduc 150
licorice 117, 207
limestone 130
line-snapping 174
Li Po 71
lips 16, 156–157, 210
Little Sparta 225
logography 39
Loki 113, 143, 188,
    247, 251
longing 5, 24

M

machine 29, 171, 208
MAGA 249
Magellanic 249
magnet 38, 247
Magritte, René 192
Mallarmé, Stéphane 32
many-forgotten 178
Mao Zedong 31, 128
map 33, 40, 72, 90, 101,
    127, 180, 187, 238, 250
margin 2, 154
Marine Drive 64
Marlatt, Daphne 35
marmot 128
Marx, Karl 17, 107
Massachusetts 62, 148
material 12, 211
Matisse, Henri 138
meaninglessly 142
measure 78, 106, 115, 117,
    143, 175, 243
Meloids 133
Melville, Herman 60
membrane 46
memo-cloud 111
memory 2, 15, 43, 47, 60,
    71, 73, 77, 81, 93, 97, 112,
    114, 116–117, 121, 132,
    136–137, 143, 171, 181,
    189, 208, 221–222, 230,
    241, 243, 250–251
me-ness 183

mescal 76
messenger 63
Métis 175
Mexico 207
midden 135
middle-voice 17, 57, 64
mind 4–5, 8, 11, 15, 22, 34,
    38, 40, 42–43, 48, 60, 64,
    68, 76, 84, 90–91, 102,
    104, 132, 143, 155, 158,
    165, 178, 187, 190, 197,
    222, 235, 238, 245–246
mindingness 132
miscegenate 175
modernists 45
moireéd 199
Molson 170
mongrel 175
Moodie, Susanna 49
moon-pear 136
Mori-san 23
morphologically 17
morphology 11, 45, 153,
    178
morphophonic 134
mother 35, 58, 135, 174,
    221
mountaining 112
Mount Fuji 68
mouthings 7
music 2, 5, 17, 19, 75,
    100–101, 104–105, 128,
    133, 209, 222, 224, 248
muzak 198

N

nacre 240
narrative 79, 100–101, 108,
    123, 127, 185, 222
nation 49, 98, 127, 178,
    193, 231
nature 12, 165, 196
nemo-fibres 175
nest 20, 80, 132–133, 140
Nichol, bp 132, 212
Nietzsche, Friedrich 192
noctiluca 83
noping 42
notation 4, 71, 111
noumen- 222
nunning 135

O

oars 186
Oaxaca 60
Obit 222
ocean 10, 22, 34, 39, 126, 135, 205, 209, 229, 231, 236, 249
Octopus Books 199
Odysseus 92
O'Hara, Frank 165
Okanagan 43
Olson, Charles 30, 38, 77
On Lok 180
optopotent 105
orange-robed 81
Oregon 57, 111, 248
osprey 20–21
ostranenie 13, 224

P

pachinko 203
Pacific 31, 37–38, 71, 205, 248
packthread 175
Palladium 151
Palmer, Samuel 55
Panopticon, Steve McCaffery 89
paradigmatic 173, 222
paradise 55, 140, 144, 148, 218
paraph 148
Paris 29, 137–138, 144
path 49, 93, 105
Pauline 84, 172
Pausanias 93, 95
pawprint 192
Pearagraphs 132
Pearl Harbor 194
Penner-Bancroft, Marian 171
Penner, Susan 171
Perry, Sam 39
Persian 122, 147, 174
phantopoeic 226
pickerel 188
pictographed 127
Piikani 218
piss-fir 168
Placitas 224
plant 156, 211, 231

Plato 11, 97, 153, 230
Pleistocene 33
Plunkett 77
Pocatello 68
poet 31, 100, 134–135
poetry 37, 45, 55, 64, 94, 117, 166, 177–178, 250
Point Grey 38
Porsena, Lars 167
Porter, Cole 198
potatoes 160–161, 206
Pound, Ezra 57
practice 16, 19, 82, 158, 193
prairie 30, 144, 185, 195, 224, 232
preaction 117, 135
print 14, 77
proprio 136, 143
Prynne, Jeremy 88
puck 183
pudeur 58, 106
punct 98

Q

Qu'Appelle 19
quaquaversal 117
Québec 90, 100, 148
quipment 220
Quito 250

R

racism 122
radio 194, 203, 226
récits 156
remembering 8, 44, 222, 229
remittance 248
remuda 116
returns 35, 40, 71
revolution 25
rice 106, 109, 111, 159, 180
r-i-f-f 200
riprapped 104
river 10, 22, 31, 69, 71, 75, 82, 90, 93–94, 97, 111–112, 117, 125, 133, 145, 148, 178, 219, 232, 236–237, 245, 250–251
rock 22, 31, 57, 65, 69, 72, 76, 80, 122, 124, 145, 176, 198, 217, 249
Rockies 99

Rodefer, Stephen 22, 177
rope-a-dope 174
Rouveyre, André 138
runic 37

S

sacred 93–95, 175
Safeway 137
Sally 20
salmon 10, 125, 135
Salt Lake City 203
saṃsāra 79
Sandia 207
Santa Fe 224
Sapir–Whorf hypothesis 184
Saskatchewan 232
Saussure, Ferdinand de 40
saxophoning 86
Scapes 72
scatology 89
Schrödinger, Erwin 103
Schumann [frequency / resonance] 21
Schwitters, Kurt 192
Scouting 216
Scree-sure 110
Seattle 79, 171
sedimentary 46
seismal 156
sememes 33
sensorimotor 174
sentence 1–2, 11, 13, 64, 94, 187, 217, 222, 246
shakuhachi 132
Shanghai 23, 151
sheh 179
Shinto Gate 141
shit 24, 79, 89, 96
Shklovsky, Viktor 13
shore 23, 55, 60, 63, 82–83, 169, 176, 185, 203, 209, 234–235
Shore, Jane 55
Siegler, Karl 107
sigh 1, 31, 133, 139, 141, 143, 145, 154, 236
silence 20, 27, 57, 65, 91, 93, 99–100, 111, 134, 144, 184, 222, 231, 237
siped 111